ADULT STUFF

THINGS YOU NEED
TO KNOW TO
WIN AT REAL LIFE

ROBERT BOESEL and **MATT MOORE**

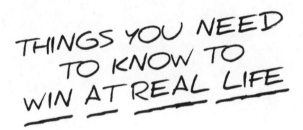

sourcebooks

Published by Sourcebooks, Inc.
P.O. Box 4410, Naperville, Illinois 60567-4410
(630) 961-3900
Fax: (630) 961-2168
www.sourcebooks.com

Library of Congress Cataloging-in-Publication Data
Boesel, Robert.
  Adult stuff : things you need to know to win at real life / Robert Boesel and Matt
Moore.
     pages cm
  (trade paper : alk. paper) 1. Adulthood—Humor. 2. Conduct of life—Humor.
I. Moore, Matt. II. Title.
  PN6231.A26B64 2016
  818'.602—dc23

                              2015030600

              Printed and bound in the United States of America.
                    VP 10 9 8 7 6 5 4 3 2 1

Contents

Introduction

Congratulations on buying this book! If you're reading this, you're most likely a fantastic twentysomething who still has that "new adult smell." Fresh from college graduation, you can't wait to move on to the next stage of your life: adult-hood! But it's scary and exciting, and you're not quite sure what to expect. Thankfully, since you're a smart, attractive, professional go-getter, you went searching for answers on a bookshelf. And it just so happened that this book was on the shelf. What are the chances? It must be fate.

So now you have our little book, and you're hoping it will provide some concrete advice on how to become a fully functioning adult. Maybe this book will even tell you *everything* you've ever wanted to know about the mysterious "real world." Then with all your questions answered, you'll attack life with enlightened gusto. You'll make all the right choices, get the job of your dreams, find a wonderful significant other, and secure a limitless future. Everything great in your life will happen because you decided to read our amazing book.

We're sorry to break it to you, but…

This book is not that amazing.

But it'd be so great if it were, right? Don't get us wrong—it's pretty good. We spent a fair amount of time putting it together, and there *is* some solid stuff in here. But it's not going to solve all of your problems about becoming a fully functioning adult (sorry). Why? Because we're barely functioning adults ourselves. We're not qualified to advise you on how to negotiate a raise or how to cook a nutritious dinner in under twenty minutes. Honestly, we're not qualified in any field that could remotely help you with how to begin your adult life. *Hang on!* Don't put the book down yet. What we *do* have is the real-world experience of living through our twenties, and we have the scars to prove it.

We were once like you: ready to take on the world, convinced that with just a little moxie and luck, everything was going to work out exactly the way we thought it would. Then we entered the real world and it slapped us around, took a cigarette break, and slapped us around some more.

Only in hindsight did we realize our biggest problem. We were expecting everything to work out perfectly all the time. We thought we were entitled to a complication-free decade of frivolity because that's what TV and movies led us to believe. Oh, what fools we were. Had we approached our twenties with realistic expectations, we could have saved ourselves undue disappointment and enjoyed the ride so much more.

So yeah, this might not be the greatest book ever written, but some of our advice is halfway decent. In baseball terms, this book is a double. It's not a grand slam, but it's also not an out. It's like most things: somewhere in between. And like most things, with the right perspective, this modest success could make you feel satisfied. And really, that's how you win at life.

We're going to reset your expectations about adulthood back to reality. Like older brothers who already lived through what you're experiencing, we're going to dish out some tough love so you don't make the same mistakes we did. And just like actual older brothers, we may make you laugh or hurt a little. We'll try to have equal parts "tough" and "love," so be cool and don't tell Mom.

Oh, and we're not going to tell you to "lean in" or that "Anything is possible in your twenties with these simple steps!" Come on. Not everything in life is possible. Not everything in life will be perfect. But if you approach it the right way, you may discover that an imperfect life is better than a perfect life, because that means you're actually living one.

EMPLOYMENT

Internship

Perfect World

You somehow landed yourself an internship. It's unpaid, but your foot is firmly in the door. And where does that door lead? To your shimmering future of success at this company. With your hard work ethic, you'll be able to impress your superiors in no time. You know those filing cabinets better than you know your own reflection—the *Mc*'s come after the *M*'s, and all the *XYZ*'s share the same folder. You are the office master of skill and alphabetical organization—a modern Michelangelo, and these files are your manila-colored *David*. Your boss looks over your tireless labor and nods in proud celebration, then calls out your craftsmanship before an office-wide standing ovation. As Jill from HR adds your name to the Employee of the Month board, your boss hands you a box of business cards. Welcome to the team, intern.

Get Real

You think they're going to hire the intern for a big-person job just because you can file? An eight-year-old can alphabetize (and probably do it faster), so don't start putting in your vacation requests quite yet. You are an intern because the job market is sluggish and no company wants to pay for another full-time employee, even one with a brand-spankin'-new bachelor's degree. And job experience is job experience, even if it's unpaid or at minimum wage. Welcome to the bottom of the ladder, kid. Brace yourself, because you're about to get stepped on.

You vs. Eight-Year-Old

Are you good at cleaning up messes? No, that's not a euphemism for "solving important problems." But can you grab some paper towels and clean up the coffee that spilled in the kitchen? Your coworkers know that's not your job, but then again no one really knows what you do. They're going to ask you to clean up the spill so they can at least see proof that you do *something*.

While you're not interning to learn how to be a janitor (you may not be qualified for that position either), just keep your mouth shut and do what is asked of you. The only way to be given more responsibilities is to be a team player. In this case, you're less of a player and more of the water boy who hands out the towels on the sideline, but at least you're a part of the organization, so clean up those (literal) messes and stay in the game.

Finally, after an eternity of filing reports and cleaning up espresso mishaps, someone will eventually notice your hard work and take you under his or her wing. While this may look like your opportunity for a fun *Lethal Weapon* "veteran cop/rookie cop" learning experience, this is going to be more of a "veteran cop stomps on rookie cop" *Training Day* experience. You're in for some long, gritty hours learning about the business from a jaded insider's perspective.

But take comfort; making it through this tough initiation phase is how you're going to learn the most about this business and even more about yourself. Knowing how much crap you can endure without giving up will help when it comes to working real jobs, meeting deadlines, and achieving life goals. Success never happens without hardship, so if this internship is hard, try to remember it's going to benefit you later.

Just Do This

Internships are a humbling introduction to the world of real business. If you can navigate this minefield of corporate culture, you'll be prepared when it's your time to enter the actual job market. More importantly, you'll add some actual business experience to your featherlight résumé, which will help you get a job faster than your college GPA ever will. An internship is a challenging place to start if you're not used to being talked down to, but try to set your fragile ego aside and use the internship as an opportunity to eventually move a step up that very tall corporate ladder.

Interview

Perfect World

Your eye contact is confident and warm. Your laugh is sincere and genial. Your quip about the weather could fit in a *Late Night* monologue. You have a résumé full of impressive work experience. Now all you have to do is stick the landing with a firm handshake, and you'll get that employment gold medal. And the judges give it a perfect ten! Congratulations interviewee, you just got an adult job!

Get Real

At least, that's what you imagine when you practice your interview in the company's bathroom mirror before your meeting. If your reflection were handing out jobs, you'd certainly be starting on Monday. Unfortunately, a skeptical look is the only thing you're going to get from talking to yourself in the restroom, so before you do anything unforgivably weird, go back to the lobby and take a seat.

Believe it or not, nailing a big job interview has less to do with your education and prior experience and more to do with just convincing the HR department that you're not a murderer. Every little eccentric thing you do while in their office will count against your final score, and talking to yourself in the restroom is a pretty big red flag. So keep your fantasies to yourself before someone has to call the cops.

What Employers Are Judging You On

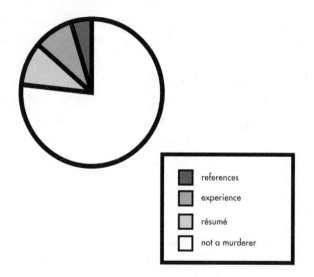

- references
- experience
- résumé
- not a murderer

When it's finally time to greet the person who will interview you, it's essential to give a good handshake. It should be professional and self-assured, but that doesn't mean to go Muscle Beach and squeeze too hard. Your grandpa was right when he scared you into believing people will judge you on a weak handshake. Still, you don't need to put your potential employer in a cast just to convince him or her you're management material. Try to practice on your friends before the interview if you're not sure about your squeezable strength. Make an employer judge you based on your résumé, not your ability to dislocate fingers.

The interview seems to be going well, and the HR director is impressed with your previous work experience. Too bad you made most of it up so you could land this interview. Sure, "waiter at Applebee's" doesn't sound that remarkable when you're trying to land a real job, but neither does "guy who lied about being a restaurant manager" when your potential employers check your references. Nothing says "crazy person" quite like a pathological liar, so do yourself a favor and stick to the truth, as lame as it may be.

Well, either the HR manager finds your fresh-out-of-college eagerness adorable or the company must be short-staffed because it sounds like they could use you. Just don't blow it when you smile, shake her hand, and thank her by name for her time. Thank her by name…name! Crap, what is her name? You don't remember because you've been focusing on the web of lies covering your résumé.

While it may not seem like a big deal, remembering someone's name can be the difference between a cushy, white-collar job and working in retail. Of course, when you're nervous, you can't remember everything, but blanking on an important person's name may be the cherry on top of your fairly suspicious behavior sundae. If you can't think of it, avoid calling attention to that fact. Just be overly exuberant in your farewell when you thank her for her time. That will keep her from noticing the incredible blunder you just committed.

Just Do This

Job interviews are tough. Don't make them harder by adding unnecessary stress to the situation. Remain calm, don't do anything strange, and stay on the side of the truth. Instead of lying about what you don't know, put the attention on everything you can do. Focus on putting your best foot forward instead of trying to keep it out of your mouth.

First Job

Perfect World

You got the college degree. You did the internship. And now you have your first job! A job that fits exactly within your field of study and sets you squarely on the path to the career you've always dreamed of. And with that fat weekly check, you'll be able to start paying off your student loan debt. *This* is what it feels like to follow your bliss.

Get Real

Aww, it's adorable you think your first job will actually apply to what you want to do with your life! Unless you majored in engineering or possess tangible skills that are, you know, actually useful in the workplace, get ready for a first job containing none of your interests. It may seem crazy to hear, but companies actually value the ability to format a spreadsheet *more* than the ability to recite eighteenth-century prose. Who would work in such an uncivilized office? You would, kind sir or madam, because you are in need of money.

No, your first job will not be your dream job. Your first job will be *a* job, and it will pay *some* money. And you should be grateful for that, because as of right now, you are not qualified for the awesome job you really want. You may have dreams of being the next Don Draper of the advertising world, but Don Draper didn't become Don Draper at twenty-two. He had to live a lot before that happened. Yeah, he's a fictional character, but you get the point.

And if you were a humanities major at a private university, you'd better be sitting down for this next part. There's a good chance your first job will be a regular Joe job. You might have to get a blue-collar, menial-labor position where you work with your hands instead of using your overeducated brain. (Let's hope you know how to make coffee.) Don't think you're better than this. This is the job you deserve at twenty-two, no matter how expensive your tuition was.

Who knows? Maybe you'll get lucky and find an entry-level position at a company that doesn't make you smell like a walking cappuccino. "Entry-level position" is the nice term for a job that no one wants but has to take because he or she has no skills or experience. It lives in the gray area just above "paid internship." You can proudly say you're not an intern and may even get to pay into your 401(k), but you're still doing everything an intern would do—making copies, answering phones, putting together packets. All thankless work, but necessary for a thriving business. You're a very small cog in the wheel, but hey, at least you're *in* the wheel. And the longer you can stay in the wheel, the more you can learn from the bigger cogs. You may have to get those bigger cogs coffee, but at least you're not that unimportant twentysomething barista who makes it.

Odds of Working in a Coffee Shop

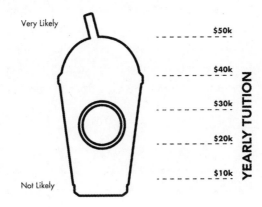

Just Do This

Here's the paradox of getting your first job: if you don't have any experience, companies won't want to hire you. But for you to gain experience, a company has to hire you…and that's when you have a catch-22 stroke. So take whatever job you can get. People who skip the soul-crushing "paying your dues" step in their careers don't appreciate how good they have it and therefore treat everyone below them like crap. Since you will start at the bottom rung, you'll learn key lessons about empathy, discipline, and drive that immediately successful people will never fully understand. So when you're Big Cog and order your coffee from Little Cog, you won't yell at him for the shortage of foam on your latte. You once were a little cog too and therefore are not an asshole.

And even if your first job sucks—like, realllllly sucks *hard*—it will still help you reach your second job. Your second job might not be your dream job either, but it will still help you reach your third job. And by that point, you just might be on the dream career path. But you have to start somewhere, so take down those lunch orders and do it with a smile.

Happy Hour

Perfect World

Work sucks. But man, those two-dollar pints and three-dollar well drinks across the street do not. From nine to five you may be an underpaid drone just waiting to die, but at the bar from five to seven, you're the wealthiest person in town and you're going to live forever! Loosen your neck-tie, grab your coworkers, and punch that clock right in its big, dumb corporate face. It's happy hour, baby, and you're never working again!

Get Real

Hey, as long as you're trying to get fired, you may as well send a photocopy of your ass to your boss too. It'll look just like the drinking you're about to do with your coworkers: not pretty. Your coworkers aren't your friends. They're just the people you tolerate when you're stuck at work. Many of your coworkers may be nice people, but if you don't trust them with your log-in credentials, you shouldn't be drinking around them. They're like a Mafia family dressed in office attire. Someone could be a rat. This is the wrong crowd to tell how you really feel about work, and if that's what you do when you start drinking, you should not be here.

Alcohol makes stupid people do stupid things, like talk shit in front of coworkers.

Alcohol Conversation Converter

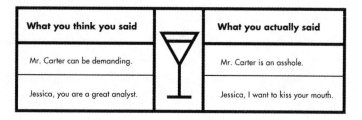

What you think you said		What you actually said
Mr. Carter can be demanding.		Mr. Carter is an asshole.
Jessica, you are a great analyst.		Jessica, I want to kiss your mouth.

While your real friends will enjoy the subtle beauty of that joke you made about your boss, your coworkers will only remember the incriminating part—and will likely repeat it at the most inopportune moment. It's much safer to hide your biting, observational humor from the office and instead talk about that funny cat video one of your coworkers sent to everyone.

Or perhaps your misunderstood sense of humor will come off as charming and you'll finally convince your work crush that you're a datable human being! You never know until you try, but trust us—*happy hour is not the time or place to make your move.* For one thing, if your work crush isn't into you, you run the risk of getting gunned down in front of everyone. The only thing worse than having unrequited feelings for a work crush is having all your coworkers know you have unrequited feelings for a work crush. Happy hour can be a place for subtle flirting, but it is not a place to lay it all out. If you're feeling it, use this time to gauge interest and save your "A game" for a more private setting where you don't have to worry about the prying eyes of HR.

Just Do This

Work happy hours are the "Reply All" of social outings. Everyone is going to see whatever you put out there. As with all events involving coworkers, moderation is key. Stick to a strict one-drink limit, and excuse yourself once the glass is empty. And know your audience well enough to save any anti-work comments for those who can keep your confidence. Remember: the best happy hours are the hours you happily spend with your *actual* friends, whether they work with you or not.

Happy Hour Merit Badge

The Hot Receptionist

Perfect World

You see her every day as you enter the office, flawlessly coiffed and postured in a swivel chair: the hot receptionist. When she's not answering the phone, she gives you a big smile that starts your day off right. When she *is* answering the phone, she still manages to give you a flirtatious wave as you pass and try to pretend like you weren't slowing down to allow her time to acknowledge you. Now it's lunch, you're making small talk with her, and you two are vibing like crazy. Better have the fire department on call, because these smoldering stares you're exchanging are about to set the office ablaze.

That's it. You can't endure the sexual tension anymore. Time to move this casual flirtation to the next level. It's time to ask her out. What's the harm in dating her? You're both young and like to have fun. There's nothing wrong with seeing a movie or grabbing some tacos after work. And if it goes somewhere, even better. You'd have a precious meet-cute story to tell your kids. Yep, asking her out could be the start of something wonderful.

Get Real

More likely, asking out the hot receptionist will be the start of something uncomfortable. She could just be nice to everyone, so you've misread her signals and she turns you down. If she does, it might sting at first, but be thankful for her rejection. The hot receptionist just saved you from the biggest land mine in the workplace: the office romance. Office romances are treacherous—so treacherous that HR has rules against them. Sure, it worked out for Jim and Pam from *The Office*, but even that took seven years and 187 episodes. But it could happen, yeah. Happily ever after and all that. But if it doesn't…

If it doesn't work out, you will still have to see the hot receptionist *every single day you go to work*. Multiple times a day, probably. And it will be awkward. Even if your relationship ends amicably, it's still going to be awkward. And if it ends poorly? Forget it. You'll have to reroute your path to the bathroom just to avoid the lobby.

And of course your coworkers are going to find out about you two dating. It'll be the most exciting news in the office since the boss installed that Keurig coffee machine. Now you'll have to walk past smirks and whispers everywhere you go. After leaving the copy room, you'll have to explain to a grinning Stacy that you really were just making copies. Then Stacy will do that stupid, all-knowing nod and say, "Sure you were." You don't want to deal with that, so don't date someone in the office. Stacy was annoying enough before having this on you.

Just Do This

Look, everyone gets it. The hot receptionist is, well…hot. And she's probably got a great personality too. She seems to have everything you want in a dating partner. But the odds of successfully dating her are basically the same as shooting the moon. Unless you end up marrying this person or one of you moves to a different office, the relationship isn't heading toward a good place. It might seem like a great call, but that's one call you should put on hold.

Credit Cards

Perfect World

It's getting harder to cover all your expenses. If you made a little more at your job, you'd be fine. But you've only been working there for three weeks, and it seems a little early to ask for a raise. Why not put some of your expenditures on your credit card? That'll keep you going. If you just pay the minimum every month, you'll be fine. Then, when you get that baller job in a couple months—which is totally gonna happen—you'll be swimming in dough. You can deal with all this credit card business then, between your spa treatments and trips to Aspen.

Get Real

Come on, you know better than this. Credit cards are dangerous, especially when you're poor. Why do you think those companies make so much money? Hint: It's because of broke-ass twentysomethings like you. Credit card companies are legal loan sharks. When they're done with you, you won't have a financial leg to stand on. Interest rates can legally go up to 29.99 percent. That means every time you buy something with money you don't have, you're potentially paying about a third more than the list price. So, that four-dollar coffee is really five dollars. And that $600 flat screen is really $800. Yes, HBO looks better on a larger screen, but your bank account looks better when there's money in it.

Just Do This

Here comes one of the least sexy topics in life: making a budget. It's up there with re-grouting the bathroom and attending a wake. It's not complicated. We know it's not, because we just Googled "good budget for twentysomethings pie chart" and found this on the first page of the search results:

> Household – 35 percent
> Life – 25 percent
> Transportation – 15 percent
> Savings – 10 percent
> Debt repayment – 15 percent

Your debt repayment should only demand 15 percent of your entire budget. You're probably already paying off student loan debt and your car. You don't need another interest payment because you bought the box set of *The Golden Girls*. Food, clothing, and shelter—these are things you need to survive. In tight times, these items are fine to charge on credit cards. But "food" doesn't mean dinners at trendy restaurants, "clothing" doesn't mean designer shoes, and "shelter" doesn't mean a weekend stay in a junior suite.

Credit cards are better thought of as a temporary solution to an emergency situation. If you have no other option, you can use them, but remember you're going to have to pay it all back. When you have access to a credit limit that rivals your monthly salary, it's easy to feel like you're flying first class, but in reality all that debt is only going to buy you a first-class ticket to rock bottom.

Business Trip

Perfect World

There's a suitcase under your desk, a plane ticket in your pocket, and a pair of slip-on loafers on your feet. Sure, right now it's a normal day at the office, but a few short hours and an x-ray screening later, all that is going to change. The boss could have asked anyone to go, but just "anyone" doesn't have what it takes. She wants you to represent the firm to the world, and she's prepared to make it worth your while: business class flight, corporate expense account, and a suite at the Plaza. Congratulations, business professional. Welcome to the big leagues. You're going on a business trip.

Get Real

Maybe those perks come to other, more established employees. But you're probably about to board the economy class, four-hour layover version. Instead of coasting through an easy week sitting at your office desk, you'll have to fly middle seat between a chubby guy and a screaming infant all the way to San Clevelandburg. Not to mention the endless meetings, corporate jargon marathons, and stressful dinners with local blowhards in the field. Sorry, buddy, but the only one getting the business on this trip is you.

Business Trip Airline Seating Chart

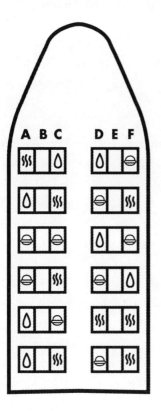

Seat Map Key

☐ Available

⊖ Space Invaders

◊ Crying Babies

𝖘𝖘 Farters

It may seem like a miracle that the bigwigs chose you, a relative unknown, to represent their highly successful company, but their decision may be less of a miracle and more of a practical choice. You may be going because you're just the right mix of "talented" and "expendable," which makes you the savior of the firm's bottom line.

Yes, you're important and somewhat competent enough to represent the main office on the road, but that also means you are not essential to the inner workings of the main office. But if you prove yourself on this business trip, soon enough you could be the person assigning this annoying task to other unsuspecting go-getters.

Whew! Those meetings were excruciating, but now you've earned yourself some after-hours fun. *Warning*: you are about to go out with professional drinkers. Please proceed with caution. These guys working in the field may look like you (aside from their white socks with dress shoes), but they live in a boring city. And what boring cities lack in culture and entertainment they make up for in power drinking. Do not think you can hang with these guys. Trying to drink with them is like trying to make a full-court basket. You may make it by the end of the night, but you're going to have to take a lot of shots. If you're not ready to fall asleep in a foreign bathtub mumbling incoherently, tell these guys you're a bit light-headed and cut out after dinner.

Just Do This

A business trip is called a business trip for a reason: you're still on the clock. If it were supposed to be fun, it would have a better name, like a "vacation." The best way to handle a business trip is to be prepared and professional so you can dazzle all the bigwigs back at the office. Of course, doing too good a job on the road might earn you more business trips, but it might also better your chances of promotion so you never have to visit any of these Podunk towns again. Then when you're a premium asset at the company, they'll save you for real trips to real cities, where your hard work will earn you a real expense account. That's when business trips can be real fun.

Work Christmas Party

Perfect World

The year is drawing to a close, and you're at the top of your game. You caught that discrepancy in the numbers from the second quarter and saved your company millions. Now you have the bigwigs' attention, and your department head has been awfully nice in anticipation of your promotion. Things are really shaping up for you at the firm. Better seal the upper management deal this weekend at the work Christmas party. Go ahead and alert the National Guard, because Winter Storm *You* is about to blow in.

Get Real

The cliché about work Christmas parties is as real as your firm's online content filter. All your hard work and good reputation can be wiped out as soon as your necktie makes the drunken transformation to a headband. You've put in too many hours to be *that* guy. Seriously.

Employment Necktie Indicator

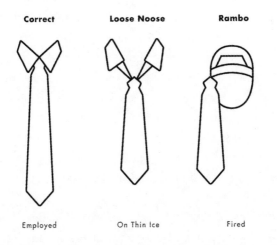

Correct	Loose Noose	Rambo
Employed	On Thin Ice	Fired

The work Christmas party may seem like the perfect time to relax and introduce the work crowd to the *real* you, but unfortunately this is still a work function, so the *real* you is going to have to stay in the *real* world outside the office. Even though this party is set in a location outside the office, the fact that work people are present makes it a work function. The only "relaxed" thing here is the cut of that IT guy's khakis, so keep up the professional facade and don't do anything stupid.

Good news! There's an open bar…but that doesn't mean it's open for *you*. Remember: your boss is watching, and he's taking notes on who drinks too much. He would love for you to lose control so he can always have something over you. That way, if you're ever on the chopping block, he has more than one reason to let you go. Open bars are only truly open at weddings or college graduations. You know, actual celebrations. This is really just an opportunity for the boss's wife to show off her new gown.

But you need a couple drinks to hit on Erica from accounting! She's so pretty she makes you nervous, especially when she smiles with just her eyes. Maybe this is a perfect time to make your move. You crack a joke about the new Xerox machine, and in minutes you'll be driving her home.

This might be a good idea *if* you didn't work together. C'mon, unless you work at a skateboard company, no one's getting laid tonight.

And if they do, it's going to become a scandal and then someone has to get fired. Just smile at Erica from across the room and *ignore* the Michael Jackson song that's playing...

Don't dance. Don't dance. Whatever you do, don't dance. Nothing is going to hurt your career more than spinning around on the dance floor. There's a reason no break-dancer has ever been featured in *Forbes* magazine, and nothing you're about to do is ever going to change that. Booze tirades can be forgiven, but bad dancing is *forever*.

Just Do This

The work Christmas party can be a good place to relax and enjoy your coworkers on your way to a nice Christmas bonus, but it can also be a good place to slur, dance, or puke your way out of a nice Christmas bonus. Leave your desire to impress work people at work and just keep it light. Preset a drink limit and a time to make a moderately early exit. The only thing worse than being the drunk guy is being the guy who's there way too long. Just make an appearance, shake the boss's hand, and begin plotting your exit strategy. Make it look like you're a man who has a fast-paced, demanding life outside work. This idea may seem counterintuitive to enjoying yourself at a party, but it's a good way to ensure you still have a job on Monday.

Quitting

Perfect World

Another copy of the Jones report? *Another* copy? You've already submitted that paperwork twice without so much as a thank-you, and they want another copy of the *whole* thing? Nope. No more. You have had it with these people. This job sucks and so does your crummy paycheck, and it's about time to show Mr. Carlson that you're not going to take it anymore. "Hey, Mr. Carlson"—hold up middle finger—"how about another copy of *this*!" Today, you're quitting. And you're going out with a bang.

Get Real

Since you're starting your new job next week, go ahead and tell this job where it can go! What's that? You don't have another job lined up? Oh man, then what are you doing? Sure, quitting with gusto is as American as getting fired, but if you set this bridge ablaze before you cross it, you may end up at the bottom of the ravine. The only thing more terrible than having a crappy job is having no job at all. Make sure you have somewhere to go before you clear out your cubicle.

If the feeling of telling this job to "shove it" means more to you than future employment, keep an eye on the clock before you activate your core meltdown. Remember: if it's anytime between eleven thirty and one thirty, also known as "lunch," you need to pump the brakes and stall for time. Telling off your boss and everyone in the office is only effective if your boss and everyone in the office are actually *in the office*. If you pull the trigger over the lunch hour, no one will really know what happened, and they may just think you stole a sandwich and got fired. Hell no! If you don't want Terry to go on thinking his humming didn't annoy you or let Katherine off the hook without telling her you don't give a shit about her kids, be aware of the time when you decide to take your stand.

Like an NSFW link in your search history, flipping out at work can't be ignored once your boss sees it. You only have one shot at this, kid, so don't screw it up.

If people are out to lunch and can't hear your tirade, you could always send a quick email to the entire office detailing your feelings. But move fast, because IT may already be in the process of blocking your access credentials. IT always knows everything before it happens, and they're going to be poised to shut you out before you can take a shot at stealing anything important. At the first sign of dissent with your job, create and save a prewritten manifesto in your drafts folder. Then when the time comes for you to walk, you can send that email without breaking your stride to the door.

Quitting Proverb

"If a tree quits over lunch, does anybody hear it?"
Confucius, CEO

Just Do This

Quitting can be a great way to assert yourself or settle scores with some horrible coworkers, but just like reapplying for unemployment, you need to plan that shit out. Sleep on your decision to quit and make certain this is really what you want. Quitting in the heat of the moment with expletives and property damage is exhilarating, but it will affect your ability to get another job. Giving your previous boss the finger is usually a pretty big red flag for potential employers, so this may not be the best move for your long-term career.

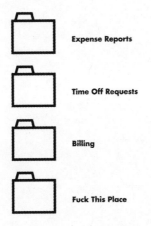

Expense Reports

Time Off Requests

Billing

Fuck This Place

While not as powerful as flipping a desk on your way out the door, the standard two-week notice allows you to avoid answering uncomfortable questions at your next job interview. Plus, you can use those two weeks to burn through some paid sick days, which will really stick 'em where it hurts.

DOMESTICITY

Adult Apartment

Perfect World

You're a young professional now! You've got a job and every-thing. And you know what would go great with that gainful employment? Somewhere to live. You're too old to crash on a friend's couch anymore; you need a place you can call your own. Yes sirree, there's nothing that would go better with adulthood than your first adult apartment. So throw the John Belushi posters away and put that marijuana flag in storage because you're moving into your beautiful dream apartment, straight out of an episode of *Friends*!

Get Real

The only part of the *Friends* set where you might be able to live is the janitor's closet on their soundstage. Your first adult apart-ment won't be a gorgeous place perfect for wine and cheese nights. You're broke. Your job pays you a yearly salary less than the yearly tuition at your fancy alma mater, and you definitely don't have the credit score or the money to lease some hip loft in that burgeoning downtown neighborhood. Sure, it might seem edgy and gritty enough for you to afford, but that's just the residual post-gentrification grime. Notice how all the remaining graffiti lacks gang references or controversy of any kind? That neighborhood is the Disneyland version of urban decay.

The *actual* edgy and gritty neighborhoods…those will be more in your price range. Imagine a street where your concerned parents would never want to visit. That's where your first adult apartment will be. On your street, police patrols will be a daily occurrence, like a friendly neighbor walking his dog. Those helicopters flying overhead at night? They're like your songbirds. And that discolored stain in the hallway? Just don't ask. It's better that way.

Visual Guide to Neighborhood Gentrification

Gentrified

Graffiti will be more art than vandalism, usually stenciled, typically sociopolitical. You won't live here.

Up-And-Coming

Graffiti will be strongly visual, often vibrant, showcase for the neighborhood's talent/promise. You could live here with a roommate.

Dicey

Graffiti will be illegible, hastily done, extremely off-putting. This is where you can afford to live.

Forget accent walls. Just hope your bedroom *has* walls. And is legally considered a bedroom. With a couple pieces of plywood and nails, a sneaky landlord can portion off a section of your living room and call that new windowless area in the corner a "bedroom." Your ceilings will not be vaulted; they will most likely be of the popcorn variety. You'll wonder if the texture resembles asbestos, which will lead to a stressful evening spent trying to confirm your suspicions online. And the closest you'll get to brushed-metal fixtures will be tasting rust in your water, thanks to the landlord's shoddy plumbing job. You have a car? Great! Make sure you know how to parallel park on the street, because you're not going to get a parking space with your unit.

Just Do This

This all may seem harsh, but never fear. If you avoid eye contact, don't wear rival gang colors, and wait five to ten years, your pregentrified neighborhood might even get declawed like that area you want to live in now. And if possible, don't ask your parents to pay for a nicer place to live. You're an adult; you shouldn't continue to live rent-free because of your parents. Yes, with their help you could stay in a better neighborhood. You might even get within spitting distance of that *Friends* apartment. But then you would deprive yourself of character-building experiences that will dramatically change your perception of the world. Like, actually learning to live on your own.

Enjoy this first adult apartment for all it is. Revel in the bad landlord who took six months to fix a broken door. Savor the unreliable washer that leaves your clothes a soaking wet ball half the time. This will all be great story fodder for those cocktail parties you'll attend in your established forties. Besides, you're in your twenties. You don't deserve nice things yet.

DIY Repairs

Perfect World

You've had enough. That kitchen faucet has been leaking for over a week. You told your landlord and she said she'll send someone over, but that was five days ago. You're through waiting for Barry to squeeze you into his repair schedule. You don't need him! You're a smart, capable, independent individual living all on your own! Time to break out that unused tool set you got for high school graduation and do it yourself.

Get Real

But…what do you know about fixing a sink? Oh, that's right, absolutely nothing. There's a reason those tools have gone unused, and that's because you don't know how to use them. Just because you watched your old man do this doesn't mean you're ready to roll up your sleeves and go all DIY. Your eagerness to fix it yourself does not mean you are *able* to fix it yourself. Just wait for Barry.

But there's a tutorial on YouTube that makes it look easy. Yes, easy for a guy with the right tools and experience. A redneck with a pencil doesn't think he's a college professor, so don't think your box of crappy tools makes you a plumber. Unless you have the right tools, you should stop before you make this any worse.

Do it yourself leak	Q
how to fix a leak am I an idiot? how to call a repairman	

Too late. You used the wrong wrench and broke the water seal on that pipe. Instead of slowing down the leak, you just made it worse. Now there's twice as much water leaking and twice as much doubt flooding your mind. Hey, Property Brothers, here's a pro tip: the first thing to do in trying to keep water from leaking is to turn the water off so, you know, it won't leak. Not only do you now have a standing pool of water under your sink, but all that water is starting to mix with those spilled kitchen cleaners and creating a cloud of pine-scented noxious fumes.

No one wants to die in a pool of their own incompetence, so always remove cleaners and potential hazards from your work area before you decide to get handy, and make sure you have adequate ventilation. Both the chemicals and your stuffy arrogance may make it hard to breathe in there.

⚠ WARNING

Caution: Contains arrogance.
Use only in well-ventilated area.

Once you can take and hold big enough breaths to get back under the sink, turn off the water valve, stop the leak, and realize you're back to zero. Only now you don't have a working faucet, leaky or otherwise. But what you *do* have is three inches of standing water in your cupboards, which won't be doing your security deposit any favors.

Just Do This

Do-it-yourself repairs may seem like an empowering idea, but in the hands of the unhandy, they can quickly escalate to a pay-for-it-yourself money pit. Sure, you may be itching to get your hands dirty, but unless it's a project you're certain you can do safely and effectively, you're better off just calling a professional. Use that DIY attitude to locate someone else to do those repairs for you, and save that fancy tool set for the next bookshelf you buy at IKEA.

Roommates

Perfect World

Your college friend is moving to the Big City too. This is going to be great! You won't have to start this new chapter of your life alone. And since you both need a place to live, why not live together? It'll be cheaper splitting utilities and rent with someone else. Plus, you'll have someone to commiserate with when you get home, someone who understands all the problems you're going through. You're both figuring out this scary new world, but when you're living with someone else, you two can figure it out *together*. You'll have late-night talks about this crazy thing called life, grazing your way through bags of Trader Joe's popcorn. You'll laugh and cry and then both decide to binge watch a show on TV until the sun comes up. This couldn't be any better.

Get Real

Actually…it *could* be better—if you didn't have a roommate. This isn't college anymore. This is the real world, and you two are adults. In college, you could stay up all night and skip class the next morning with few repercussions. In the real world, you can't skip a single day at work without risking getting fired. Unlike *college* roommates, adult roommates have the added stress of needing to make enough money to survive. You're no longer working a couple hours at the local coffee shop for beer money. You're working in order to not die, and you better believe that added anxiety will affect your home life.

You'll both be exhausted from your entry-level jobs and short tempered from all the jerks at work bossing you around. When you're the lowest on the ladder at the office, your roommate will be the only person you can kick when you're down. Or you'll have a "stress-off," trying to top your roommate with the most stressful story of the day. No one wins that game.

Unexpected outbursts will be common. Since you have no control at work, every little thing that's not to your liking at home will feel inexcusable. Your roomie leaving her shoes in the common area will be an unforgivable offense. And her strand of hair left on the bathroom sink will be the most disgusting thing you've ever seen.

Some people are great as friends but terrible as roommates. Like that one friend who's always down for a crazy adventure...but when you live with her, she brings those crazy adventures home. Or the friend who always knows the best places to eat but turns out to be one of those roommates who eats your food without asking. Then of course there's the Craigslist roommate who you don't know at all, for better and for worse. You're not at risk of losing a friendship when you live with the Craigslist roommate, but you are living with a stranger, so buckle up for some potentially creepy revelations.

Just Do This

If you want everything to be exactly the way you want in your apartment, then live alone. Living with *anyone* requires compromise, but it also requires communication. If an issue comes up with your roommate, speak directly to her about it. Passive-aggressively grunting when you see unwashed dishes in the sink does not communicate that you want your roommate to wash her dishes as well as actually telling her that. Open dialogue is key. She might not even know you have a problem with unwashed dishes until you mention it. Some people are dumb like that.

A roommate is like a pet. They can be a lot of fun, but you also have to clean up after them and deal with their crap. If you're lucky, a roommate will help more than hurt. She'll be there when you're down, watch your favorite TV shows with you, and gossip about the cute new neighbor moving in next door. Worst case, your roommate will suck. She'll undermine your confidence, invade your privacy, and make you dread going home. But hey, at least even a sucky roommate will split the rent. And with the bank account balance you're rockin', that might be just enough reason to get one.

Cleaning

Perfect World

You have a bachelor's degree now. You can't have food particles caked on your kitchen tiles. Sure, you may be living in a crappy apartment, but that doesn't mean you can't have clean countertops and swept floors. Even the most rent-controlled establishment can have a little sparkle. You're going to clean. When you're done, it'll be tidy enough for *Architectural Digest* to snap some gorgeous interior shots. "How did you get your counters so brilliantly white?" the interviewer will ask. You'll recline in your beanbag chair and chuckle at his question. "A little something called elbow grease," you'll quip, and then take a sip of cabernet, mindful not to spill on the freshly mopped floors.

Get Real

Have you ever cleaned an apartment? Like, *really* cleaned an apartment? Like, a deep clean? Like, moved the fridge and lifted furniture? This isn't going to be a quick little job. This is going to take some time. Cancel any appointments you have for the day. Seriously. Movie montages of cleaning up a park or refurbishing a house may only be a couple minutes long, but you're not in a movie. This is real life and your place is a mess.

Just Do This

Believe it or not, even filthier creatures than you are living in your apartment, so evict them with an antibacterial cleaner. To avoid the saddest high outside of huffing spray paint, wear a mask or go full desperado with a cowboy-style bandanna to protect yourself from the fumes. And unless a handsome lumberjack shows up to help, those cheap paper towels you bought won't go nearly as far as you'd think. You have a lot of grime to wipe up, so buy some dish-scouring pads to save on towels.

Bandanna Distinctions

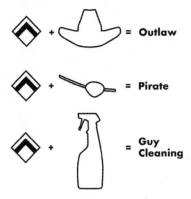

◆ + 🤠 = **Outlaw**

◆ + 👁 = **Pirate**

◆ + 🧴 = **Guy Cleaning**

If you don't know how to clean correctly, look it up online. If you still don't think you can clean correctly, pay for a professional. It's not that pricey, especially if you can split the cost with a roommate or two. In this new "shared economy" world, it's getting cheaper to pay for service industry jobs. And many cleaning companies will give you a low, low price to get you hooked. So sign up once and get someone else to do your initial deep clean. Then just do spot cleanings after. It'll be awkward making eye contact with the cleaner as she mops your filthy floors, but it's still worth it. She knows what she's doing. If you don't care about looking creepy, watch how she cleans your apartment. Then apply those professional-level techniques when you clean next time.

Even if you pay for a professional cleaner, your apartment will never look perfect. But it'll still look better than it did, and most importantly, it'll be sanitized. You'll now get to cook in a kitchen that no longer resembles a truck stop bathroom, and that's worth spending a precious Saturday on housework.

Decorating

Perfect World

Now that your apartment is clean, it's time to make it your own. A hip person like you has a unique style that needs to come out in your domicile accoutrements. Gas up that hatchback, put the backseat down, and get out to those stores. You are about to find the coolest furniture. And it'll be classy, just like you. Your rooms will flow effortlessly together, thanks to your keen eye for furnishings and use of space. When you invite that special someone over to your place, she'll take one look at your decorating and think, *This person is an adult. I want to sleep with him immediately, because he clearly has it all together.*

Get Real

You're an adult, but for your first-time decorating in the real world, you will not be buying adult-appropriate furnishings. Remember that whole no-money thing you've got going on? When thinking about your decorating budget, "shoe-string" comes to mind. So you can forget the distressed coffee table from Restoration Hardware. And avoid the Williams-Sonoma website to save yourself some heartache. Like every other postcollege first, decorating your first adult apartment is going to be about practicality and not about making your aesthetic dreams come true.

Just Do This

You really have three levels for decorating on your budget. Each one offers its own joys and disappointments.

1. IKEA/Target

Since you went to college, you already know about these wonderful stores that have basically everything you could ever want for an apartment. They're the best option for getting new items that look somewhat respectable at particleboard prices. You may end up with the same bookshelf as every other person your age, but that's better than buying a brushed-steel dining room table for the equivalent of three car payments.

2. Craigslist

Going the used route could get you better-quality items, but they might have a couple scuffs and scrapes.

If you have the time to sift through all the posts, you could go on Craigslist and find something with a little style for a cheap price. But the guy you meet in a parking lot to pick up the item will be super creepy. Chances of him driving an unmarked van? Probably about 60 percent. Bring a friend and some mace.

Types of People Selling on Craigslist

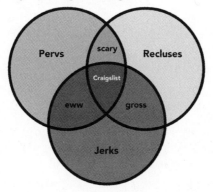

3. Thrift Stores

Thrift stores also offer unique items for your home, but once again, you have to log hours walking through the aisles in hopes of finding that perfect addition to your nest. If you spend the time, you could find some gems. You might even find a distressed coffee table, except it will actually be distressed from years of use and not from a wood treatment in a factory. This is not the option for those who want their apartment furnished quickly. But man, you can't beat the prices.

You can do some classy decorating at any price. In *your* price range though, you'll have to make concessions. But those discounted picture frames you buy at Marshalls will be filled with important people in your life, and *that's* what will make your place a home.

Getting a Dog

Perfect World

You have a nice-looking apartment, but it's starting to feel a little lonely. You're glad you don't have roommates anymore, but you miss the chatter of fellow struggling twentysomethings filling the air. Now it's just you and the quiet hum of your air purifier. Luckily, the world offers an alternative to a roommate, something a little furrier but just as good for companionship: a dog!

Getting a dog will definitely replace what you're lacking from a roommate. After a long day at work, you'll open your front door and a cheery pooch will run right up to you, overjoyed that you're back home. That's unconditional love right there, something you're not getting from your coworkers or romantic liaisons. Getting a dog will completely cure your feelings of loneliness and give you nothing but good times.

Get Real

Yes, a dog will provide companionship, but a dog will also come with more stress than a regular roommate. You didn't have to feed your roommate. Or take your roommate out for a walk. Or pick up your roommate's crap (besides that one time). A roommate is *basically* self-sufficient. Even if he doesn't have his life together yet, for the most part, you don't have to worry about him dying without your care. Not so with a dog.

A dog is a human baby that never grows up. Plus, it needs to be taken out every day and walked. Babies don't even need that. You just stick that chubby thing in a crib and you're good. Walking a dog after a nerve-racking day may relieve stress for some people, but for others it could be yet another thing to do on a list that constantly keeps growing. Which kind of person are you? Your answer should heavily affect your decision to get a dog.

Also, to be blunt, you are in no position to keep a creature alive. You're just skating by yourself. No one should have to live this unstable life with you, especially an innocent animal. If you're barely one step above destitute, now is not the time to get a dog. That dog doesn't want to live on the street, but he doesn't want to live in your apartment either.

Maybe you weren't even thinking of a dog. You're more of a cat person. But a cat has its own problems. Sure, cats are lower maintenance, but you still have to care for them. And you'll also be the person that lives alone with a cat. If that doesn't sound bad to you, go for it. But also know that every piece of fabric in your apartment will quickly be covered in cat hair, so any friend or potential hookup with a cat allergy that comes over to hang out will have to weigh your friendship or sexiness with itchy, red eyes.

Dog Living Preferences

Show Dog

Firehouse

K9 Unit

Farmhouse

Apartment

Junkyard

Your Apartment

Homeless

Dead

Just Do This

Don't get a dog. Or a cat. Not now. Figure yourself out first. Learn to manage the responsibilities you already have—and you already have a lot to manage. Then, when you think you're ready for a dog, go out and buy yourself a plant.

CUISINE

Grocery Shopping

Perfect World

You have nothing to eat at home. In the words of Mother Hubbard, that cupboard is straight up empty. You do have one solitary can of tuna, but you don't even have mayo to zest it up. And really, who eats tuna right out of the can? Somehow, another fast-food run feels childish. The fact they start making your order as you walk through the door might be a sign you're going there a little too often.

No, you're an *adult*. You need to buy some nutritious food. You need to go grocery shopping. So grab your environmentally friendly bags and head over to a place that sells more than jerky and unleaded gas. This will take no time at all. You'll quickly glide down each aisle with your cart and expertly grab food as you go. Each food selection you make will feel great, because you're now in control of your life. Let the grocery shopping begin!

Get Real

You're an adult now, so you know you have to buy green things, like vegetables. And kale. Adults eat kale. And you need to buy enough for the week so you don't have to constantly come back to the store to replenish your raw chicken breast reserves. So, how many chicken breasts is that? And do you need butter? You might still have some left. You didn't check. Butter doesn't go bad. Might as well buy some more butter. And bananas. But not too many. Last time you bought too many bananas, and half of them turned brown before you could eat them. Man, this is not fun. This is boring.

Yes, grocery shopping is boring, because now it's an errand. Grocery shopping was fun in college when you didn't have any responsibilities. It was like a food field trip. And you were never buying actual groceries. You were buying snacks and beer for a party. Who doesn't love buying that stuff? The hard choices were if you should buy cans or longnecks and which mixers go best with squeezable vodka. But now grocery shopping is an inconvenience. It's chipping away at what little free time you have, either after work when you're exhausted or on the weekend when you'd rather just watch Netflix.

As a college student, you probably were too concerned about making out with someone at your upcoming party to notice the walking adult zombies surrounding you in the grocery store. They sluggishly pushed their carts down the aisles, their deep-set eyes glazing over packages of instant oatmeal. Little did you know that would be your fate one day.

You've now learned from past trips to the grocery store that making a list is essential. So before you go, you write one that would impress any mature person. It checks all the boxes of the food pyramid or climbs the steps up the pyramid—or does whatever is considered successful in whatever shape the FDA has most recently determined is the way to tell us how to eat.

Failed FDA Food Shapes

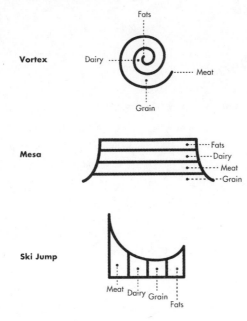

But when you get to the store, you reach into your pockets and discover they're as empty as the calories you've been eating. You forgot the list! Now you have to wing it, but you didn't eat before you left, so "nutritious you" has morphed into "hungry you," and all you're eyeing are foods that will calm your rumbling stomach. Suddenly your cart is full of ice cream novelties and Hungry-Man frozen dinners. You don't even like chicken-fried steak, but the receipt the cashier hands you says otherwise. Don't worry, you'll have another crack at grocery shopping next week. And the week after, and the week after that. Because you are going to do this *for the rest of your life.*

Just Do This

Errands aren't fun, but you have to do them. Because that's what adults do. You've been shielded from doing anything annoying your whole life. Grocery shopping is pretty low on the list of annoying adult things. Just be glad you can afford groceries. And if a couple candy bars make it into your cart, that's not a big deal. Self-medicate to deal with the newfound inconveniences of errands by having a delicious, caramel-y chocolaty treat. Then get back home. You still have to do your laundry.

Weekend Brunch

Perfect World

It's the weekend. You went out partying last night, slept in, and now you're ready to have some delicious food in the trendy Big City to get that hangover under control. Grab your friends and get goin'. It's time for weekend brunch. You'll head over to that happening Big City eatery, which is probably named something like Hash. You'll tell the hostess, "Table for eight, please."

The hostess will smile at your octet and chirp, "Right this way," seating you immediately in a plum corner booth. Your waiter will greet you promptly and really *listen* when you ask for a fruit cup substitution with your eggs Benedict. He wants you to have the best experience possible, and it shows. You are fairly confident you have never been treated as well as at this weekend brunch.

Get Real

Wait, what? Why is there a line outside Hash? Turns out, you're not the only one on a Sunday at noon who thought to get brunch. *Everyone* has the same idea, and from the looks of it, they had it before you did.

After forty minutes of standing outside, they finally call your name. Yes! You have a table…right next to the kitchen. So what if you can't hear your friends' conversation? At least you can finally sit down and look at the menu. But these prices don't seem right… How is a bowl of oatmeal nine dollars? Fifteen bucks for a frittata?! Better start draining some bottomless mimosas, because you won't want to remember how much this meal is going to cost you.

Welcome to the land of the trendy brunch, the nightclub for people who love overpriced eggs. And similar to bottle service at the club, in order to get a table, you're going to drop a lot more money than something's worth. Instead of a thousand dollars for vodka bottle service, it's going to be eighteen dollars for a breakfast burrito.

Breakfast is the most profitable meal for restaurants. Do you know how cheap eggs are? And a couple strips of bacon with some diced-up potatoes? Suuuper cheap. But thanks to supply and demand, those simple ingredients suddenly cost three times as much on the weekend. At those prices, you're better off waking up with a bowl of Cheerios and spending that money on a decent dinner.

And here's one of the most unfortunate parts of weekend brunch: paying a premium on food doesn't even grant you the right to a leisurely meal. That restaurant wants you *out*. Your table is precious real estate, and they've already gotten all the money they can out of you. That's why the waitress keeps coming by "just to check in" and see if you're ready with the bill. She wants to turn that table. And she knows figuring out how to split a check with a group is going to take nearly as long as the meal itself.

If you're planning on taking your time, you have to keep ordering food. Try ordering course by course so you can stay seated while the kitchen makes you five more pancakes. Your server might get irritated, but it will ensure you can remain at your table for longer than the amount of time you waited for it.

## How to Dress for the Club	## How to Dress for Brunch after the Club

Tight Dress	Sweatshirt
Sexy Heels	Practical Sneakers
Updo	Baseball Cap
Eye Shadow	Sunglasses
Lipstick	ChapStick

Just Do This

Weekend brunch in the Big City is a scene. If you love drama, by all means, do it. But there's a much easier eating option on the weekend. It's called breakfast. People somehow forget about this meal between Friday and Monday. The best thing about breakfast is that it includes most of the food options brunch has but without the hordes of obnoxious scenesters. And if you go to a greasy spoon diner instead of a trendy brunch spot, you can avoid ridiculous prices. So wake up a little earlier and beat the crowd. If you're still tired, there's this drink called coffee. Try it. It's usually on the breakfast menu.

Farmers Market

Perfect World

Preservatives. Pesticides. Artificial colors. *No way*. You're sick of "the Man" getting his hands on your fruits and vegetables. What happened to food just being food? You want to buy your produce the way your grandparents bought it: from the farmers. And it has to be from local farmers, not those automated Monsanto farms where they're genetically modifying everything in the ground. No, you want to buy produce from real people with real dreadlocks. You're going back to the way nature intended. There's only one place in the Big City where you can go for this agrarian dream. You're going to a farmers market. It's time to take your health back.

Get Real

Unfortunately, there's a reason it's called a "farmers market." You live in the Big City, far away from anything even remotely resembling a farm. Consequently, these farmers have to travel to the Big City to sell their organic produce. Since they're not massive factory farms, they don't have low distribution costs, which means their expensive journey will be included in that tomato you buy. Modern agriculture has its downsides, but it sure is a lot cheaper than the old-school way of growing food.

For starters, you'll notice the produce at the farmers market is a lot smaller than its genetically enhanced brethren. And in a truly dramatic twist of irony, it will cost a heck of a lot more. Yes, that modern-day inclusion of chemicals somehow makes produce cheaper and bigger, but you're willing to overlook that costly detail because you're out there interacting with the real people. *Real*, real people. Like, homeless people. Yeah, that hip bohemian you were sampling peach slices with is actually just a homeless guy, which totally makes sense, since there are all these free samples, and derelicts do blend in fairly well with the farmers market's nonconformist clientele.

Luckily, you're not alone with the Urban Outfitted and clandestine transients of the streets, because this place is crawling with like-minded business professionals. They too are looking to rise up and overthrow their supermarket overlords in the name of the organic produce revoluti—*Ohhhhh my God!* Your foot just got run over by a stroller! That's what happens when you literally stop to smell the freshly cut roses in front of a rich, suburban power mom.

Danger to Toes at Farmers Market

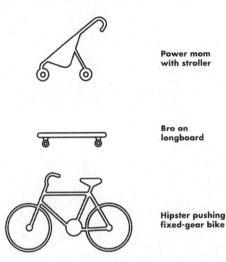

Power mom
with stroller

Bro on
longboard

Hipster pushing
fixed-gear bike

With romantic notions of farm life being replaced by the throbbing in your toes, you'll purchase a week's supply of produce to avoid having to come back, knowing full well that there's no way you'll ever eat all that kale before it goes bad.

Just Do This

While you should be eating better by buying locally sourced produce, remember this is still a business, and farmers still need to make money. Go into this knowing you will get overcharged for a ridiculously small amount of goods, and that's just the way it is. And like that fourteen-dollar eggplant in your NPR tote bag, develop a thick skin to prepare yourself for dealing with the farmers market crowd. Now with that, a hearty hats off to you for making the effort to live healthier. Just be sure your new diet doesn't poison your bank account.

Carving a Turkey

Perfect World

You're spending Thanksgiving at your girlfriend's house, and her stepdad has asked you to carve the turkey. This is a big deal. You don't want to screw it up, and you won't. Sure, you've never carved a turkey, but you've watched your old man do it for years. And it can't be that hard if that kid at the supermarket deli can do it. That guy didn't even finish high school, and he carves a bird just fine.

More importantly, this manly request means you've been accepted into your girlfriend's family. You thought you blew it at her cousin's wedding when you threw up doing the grapevine. Now Mr. Hendricks (or Todd—you can call him Todd now) is handing you the big fork and carving knife, and all has been forgiven. When they say grace, you know what you're thankful for: friends, family, and this new opportunity to prove yourself.

Get Real

Warning! Warning! Warning! All hands to battle stations! The Death Star's shield generators are still operational, and Admiral Ackbar's shouting, "It's a trap!" You've never carved a turkey, and everyone except your girlfriend knows it. You're being set up to fail!

There's a reason your old man has never let you carve the family turkey. It's a professional's job, with the smallest mistake bringing dire consequences upon Thanksgiving dinner. You're not just cutting into a bird to provide sustenance for hungry family members; you're also working with a priceless hunk of marble you must carve into a statue of perfect protein. One wrong slice, and you render the seven hours of prepping, basting, and roasting worthless. The kid at the deli knew this, and that's why he started at potato salad.

Here's the shocking truth: your girlfriend's stepdad didn't ask you to carve the turkey as an olive branch and a way into his family. He did it to expunge the benefit of the doubt that your girlfriend's mother still has about you. Todd dealt with punks like you when he was a cop in the army, and he'll be damned if you think you can puke on a dance floor and have him forget about it. Todd may be a relatively new addition to this family, but he's been there a hell of a lot longer than you have. He's only giving you this honor because he knows you'll blow it and be forever erased from future family gatherings.

And don't think that because your girlfriend's mother

pities you, she's on your side. Ha! She didn't slave away in a hot kitchen all day just so you could stand at the head of her table and piss on her *Mona Lisa*. She's sticking up for you on behalf of her daughter, but all that will change if your first cut is horizontal.

What Your Cut Says about You

On the side	Diagonal	Horizontal
"smart, son-in-law material"	"amateur, probably an idiot"	"crazy person, pedophile, criminal"

Even your girlfriend knows botching this is a deal breaker. No girl marries a man who can't carve a turkey.

Just Do This

This could be the biggest moment of your entire life…so you should get out of it. Stay on the side of courtesy and decline the request on grounds of your upbringing. Claim it's a job for the man of the house and respectfully defer to Todd. (At least he will respect your old man for putting some sense in your head.) Backing down from an obvious challenge may seem like a sign of weakness, but steering clear of danger is a sign of obvious strength. And who knows, if you hold your liquor better and compliment Todd's gun rack enough, maybe you'll make it to next year's Thanksgiving. With a year of prep time, you'll be all set for carving a turkey. And for that, you should be thankful.

Food Truck

Perfect World

You're attending that cool outdoor [music festival/art walk/ summer event], and the streets are lined with food trucks. You're hungry from all the walking and drinking, so you might as well stop at one of these traveling restaurants and grab some grub. And you've actually heard about some of these trucks on [the Internet/television/public transportation conversations you eavesdropped on], so you know they must be good. After trying their distinctive cuisine, you'll casually wipe a blob of aioli off your chin, knowing you are now on the cutting edge of the food scene.

Get Real

Okay, let's take it back a little. Food trucks aren't cutting edge anymore. They're still in vogue, but that doesn't nec- essarily mean they're good. Food trucks are a trend, and like all trends, some will be worth checking out and some won't. Don't let the spaceship decal on that food truck make you think their dumplings are "out of this world." That's just good marketing. And a cool font choice doesn't magically make their curry dog tasty. It makes their graphic designer a highly sought-after freelance employee.

Some of these food trucks aren't worth the wait, so do some research. Despite the four wheels and fuzzy dice on the rearview mirror, this isn't fast food; it's truck food. The dishes are made to order, which is great, but that means you have to wait for each order to be made. And although it may seem counterintuitive, just because you're eating food prepared in the back of a truck does not mean it's going to be cheaper. You're going to pay twelve bucks for a grilled cheese sandwich, so don't try to get full. You didn't bring enough cash for that.

Also, get ready to eat that freshly made sandwich standing up. Food trucks are mobile, which means they don't have seating. Unless you want to wake up that poor homeless guy so you can share his bench (don't), you're going to be eating this meal like the cook who made it: on your feet.

If you like taking dietary risks, then a food truck meal is the meal for you. Nothing says danger like eating something that was cooked a few feet away from a gas tank. And cooks can mishandle food on trucks, just like at normal restaurants, but chefs at normal restaurants don't also have the ability to accidentally drop food in a puddle of motor oil.

Just Do This

A food truck can be a fun way to eat something unique in an unconventional setting. That outdoor event you're attending probably doesn't have many other food options, so you're kind of stuck eating at a truck. Who knows? Maybe it will live up to the hype. But if it's not the best food you've ever tasted, at least you got some essential calories to help you survive. When you've been outdoors in the sun all day not eating anything, that's worth the extra money.

Trendy Restaurant

Perfect World

You just heard about a hip new restaurant in that up-and-coming neighborhood. All the supercool food blogs are talking about it, so you've *got* to check it out. You've always wanted to hobnob with the trendy crowd, and they *for sure* are going to be eating here. Better put on that fancy new outfit and some sexy shoes because if this place is half as stunning as the pictures on its website, you're going to want to match the interior. After all the courses arrive, each one better than the last, you'll swirl an after-dinner brandy in one of those fancy glasses people drink brandy in. When the waiter appears and asks how you enjoyed the meal, you'll bellow a satisfied groan and declare, "It was *divine*."

Get Real

As you approach the restaurant, you realize you may have overdressed. Why is this restaurant in a former airplane hangar next to the freeway? Because that's a hip place for a restaurant, *duh*.

Don't let the stray cats and human feces on the sidewalk deter you. When you get inside, it becomes much better. It's still an airplane hangar, but seeing the dark wooden interiors and other people dressed like you, now you *get* it. You feel just as cool as you hoped you would.

The hostess, dressed as a 1960s flight attendant, seats you and hands you the menu. Then your waiter, who is probably named Mason, approaches and explains that the chef's vision is a playful take on airplane food. Oh man, that's so hip. Like, people *hate* airplane food, but this is going to be, like, *good* airplane food. You better enjoy the taste of irony, because each bite you take tonight will be drenched in it.

Looking at the menu, you see that the entrées are a little pricey, but you knew that going in. And Mason says the dishes are meant to be shared, so it should work out. You and your friends order a couple plates. Pickled things, some kind of dish with pork belly, uni-topped finger foods, bone marrow served with fancy-sounding toast—you're pretty sure airlines don't serve any of these dishes on their flights, but you're reminded that's what makes this place so hip. After hearing your order, Mason suggests in the politest way possible that you order more. *More* plates? You've already ordered so many. He acquiesces, and when he returns with your food, you see why he made his suggestion.

Sheesh. Even for airplane food, these are tiny portions.

These are "small plates," the awful new standard in trendy restaurants. They used to only exist in that hipster-filled Spanish eatery import. Now every sheet metal–ceilinged new establishment is using this scam to overcharge you. Restaurants can charge you a little less than an entrée for a fraction of the food.

Small Plates Equation

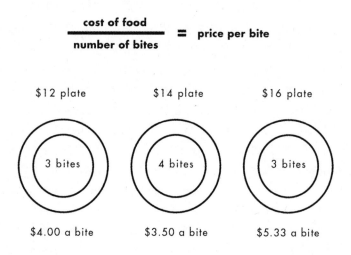

$$\frac{\text{cost of food}}{\text{number of bites}} = \text{price per bite}$$

$12 plate $14 plate $16 plate

3 bites   4 bites   3 bites

$4.00 a bite $3.50 a bite $5.33 a bite

You and your friends share the measly servings, careful to divide each tiny dish equally among all of you. Mason asks if you all want to order more. Since you may never get another reservation, you do another round and decide that if you just cancel your cable and Internet, you'll be able to afford it.

Just Do This

You want to feel cool when going out to eat, but you can't swing that kind of price tag yet. That's fine. The hip food blogs talking up this trendy restaurant have a bigger budget than you because *they eat food for a living*. You're not a professional eater, so rest easy about where you are right now budget-wise. If you want to go to the trendy restaurant and remain able to pay your rent next month, there's a fairly bulletproof strategy. A trendy restaurant usually has a decent burger with above-average fries that will fill you up and be more in line with your price point. You'll be tempted to get the truffle-infused something or other, but until you're infused with cash, stick with the burger. You'll still get to say you ate there, and you'll still be able to afford a place to live.

STYLE

Buying a Suit

Perfect World

"The name's Bond. James Bond," you say into several mirrors as you examine yourself in the world's finest suit. With spring wedding season right around the corner, it's your mission to get your *Goldfingers* all over some beautiful bridesmaids' *Casino Royales*, and this suit is your *License to Kill* all reception season long. As you motion for another glass of champagne, a flurry of assistants package your new suit and load it into the "boot" of your Aston Martin. Tell the prettiest salesclerk you need some "personal assistance" in the privacy of your dressing room, close the door, and roll credits.

Get Real

That is exactly how you'd buy a suit if you were an international spy, a playboy, or even remotely wealthy. As you are well aware, you are none of those things.

But with spring wedding season, real-world job

interviews, and adult social engagements encroaching on your daily life, you need a big boy suit to keep pace with your ever-maturing environment. So you are going to do what any tall, clueless child with very little money would do in this situation. You're going to head down to your local suit outlet to find a sensational deal on fine gentlemen's garments.

Three suits, three shirts, three belts for $299 is a great deal. It's an amazing deal. It's almost too good of a deal. You can try to ask the suit outlet sales associate how they can stay in business at those prices, but unless you want to hear an answer as mysterious as this suit's country of origin, you should save your breath.

Made from 100% colton in

Sribelbeckistan Nam

DO NOT WEAR IN DIRECT SUNLIGHT

Despite their tendency to circle you like vultures, these guys aren't there to answer your questions or to be generally helpful in any way. They're only there to ring up your purchase, collect that commission, or help you score drugs in the alley behind the store.

The good news is the suit outlet has a ridiculous number of suits on hand. The bad news is that unless you want to look like Steve Harvey, none of them are going to fit you. The only sizes available at the suit outlet are for guys who would buy a suit at a suit outlet, which from the looks of it are burly men who would be the first to die in a Bond action sequence. You won't find something stylish or form-fitting, because the tailors all did an *Oddjob* making these.

The Bond Villain Tailors

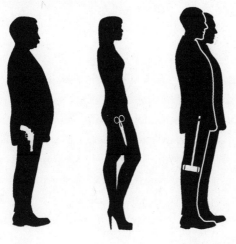

| Price Czech | Screamstress | The Brokes Brothers |

By this point, it's clear you've made a mistake in coming in here, but like that sales associate's eyebrow ring, you're in too deep and there's no getting out. You see, you made eye contact with the sales associate. In his world, you've signed an unspoken agreement to buy three suits, three shirts, and three belts. If you don't, he's going to take it very personally. Look at his eyebrow ring again and ask yourself if you're comfortable breaking a promise to this guy. If the answer is no, then the best way to avoid him following you out to your car is to respect the unspoken agreement. Just buy a suit and get out. You're going to like the way you look, because you won't be maimed with a blunt object in the parking lot. We guarantee it.

Just Do This

Buying a suit shouldn't be taken lightly. *You Only Live Twice*, but a bad suit dies a thousand deaths. Rather than getting stuck spending a little money on something you don't want, save your money and invest in a nicer suit you will be able to enjoy wearing for a while. Research the style and fit you're interested in, then go to a reputable department store with those ideas in mind. Write down details or bring photos on your phone so you can show the helpful sales associate what you're looking for.

Your effort will prove a willingness to buy, which will be met with great, attentive service. Yes, you're going to spend some extra money going this route, but at least you'll spend that money on something you enjoy wearing that was made in a country you can actually find on a map. While 007 is no stranger to getting things three at a time, rest assured that they are never his suits.

Growing Facial Hair

Perfect World

Tom Selleck. Abraham Lincoln. Questlove. What do all these men have in common? They aren't afraid to wear their furry badge of masculinity upon their chiseled mugs. You and your baby face have sat on the social sidelines long enough. It's time to take your rightful place among their manly ranks. Get ready to start opening tight-lidded jars, changing roadside flats, and running lawless desperadoes out of town, because you are now a man of distinction. You have facial hair!

Get Real

Whoa, whoa, whoa. Just because you grew some hairs out of your face doesn't mean you're automatically qualified to start splitting logs or wrestling bears, so let that tight jar lid loosen up under a warm faucet and use your strength to listen to some sound advice. Sure, almost every man can grow facial hair, but like an obese guy wearing yoga pants, just because they can doesn't mean they should.

Facial hair does have the power to instantly make you cooler, but you have to know how to do it right. A solid beard or 'stache will make you look like the toughest guy in the room, but bad facial hair or a soul patch (shudder) will make you look like someone who likes getting picked on. If you don't pick the look that's right for you, what you think might be a solid "Abraham Lincoln" may just end up being a really uncool "Hitler."

But thankfully that beard you're rockin' is really working. Everyone is looking at you! Wait, why are they laughing? Why is that guy pointing to his barren upper lip? Oh, he's gesturing to *your* upper lip…because it's covered in latte foam. Good work, doofus. You just failed Facial Hair 101: you gotta keep that baby clean! Only feral dogs look charming with food in their facial hair, so either learn to keep it tidy or get used to eating alone because no one wants to have dinner with a wild animal.

Maybe you don't have to worry about a messy beard because you can only grow a mustache. Cool. Make that 'stache happen, but just be aware you may look like a pervert. Sorry, but it's true. Thanks to a handful of child molesters' mustachioed mug shots, everyone now associates furry lip with jail time. Yeah, it's not fair, but there's nothing you and that woolly thing of yours can do about it. Your only defense is how you carry yourself with it. Tight haircut + cool style =

good. Thick clear-framed glasses + bowl cut = bad. If you're unsure on which side of the line you fall, better err on the side of caution and go close shave. There are too many nervous parents around to get this one wrong.

If you can't go full beard, mustache, or goatee—and a goatee looks good on *very* few people, by the way—you're best just to forget about facial hair. Never, under any circumstances, should you fill in your genetic shortcomings with an eyebrow pencil. This strategy only works for ringmasters and cholas' eyebrows, so unless you're in a top hat or have your boyfriend's name tattooed across your neck, you better keep a clean face (and criminal record).

Just Do This

The lure of facial hair is strong for many males, but it may be a siren's call hailing you to your social demise. If your beard or 'stache comes in thick enough to give you a mature, distinguished look, then do your part to live up to that look. Keep it clean, dress in a way that conveys a complete, stylish package, and for crying out loud, keep it trimmed. No one trusts a man with a bushy, unkempt face unless he's wearing a red suit and leaving a gift under the Christmas tree.

Getting a Tattoo

Perfect World

You're a free spirit. A lone wolf. A rebel who plays by your own rules. You see conformity and you laugh right in its khaki-wearing face. These sellouts aren't like you, and you certainly aren't like them. And you know what? It's time to give them a permanent reminder of how unique you really are. Yeah, it's time to get that sick tattoo and show the world you make bold choices. You're living in the now, and if this rad reminder on your shoulder is too real for these squares, they're gonna have to look the other way because this dope tat is here to stay!

Get Real

Yes, what you're doing may have the potential to look really cool and brand you as a hip rebel for the rest of your life. But there's also a strong risk of looking like a real chump until the day you die. You need to take this tattoo seriously. You're about to enter the sacred fraternal order of history's elite lowlifes, so if you don't want to be just another pirate, criminal, or burnout, this tattoo better be special.

Do you even know what you want permanently branded on your skin? If you don't, leave the tattoo shop *immediately*. Sure, you could ask the tattoo artist to pick something for you, but if that's the case, why don't you ask a dog to choose which of your fingers to bite off? Both will randomly mar you for life. You also could pick something predrawn off the tattoo parlor wall, but then you run the risk of getting the same tattoo as a bank robber or a prison cook. So much for individuality.

You should also think about where you're planning to put that tat. Perhaps a better question is: what kind of job are you planning *not* to have? While tattoos have become more socially acceptable, there has never been an investment banker with "HARD CORE" written across her knuckles or a kindergarten teacher with a pot leaf on his forearm. Hand and neck tattoos are basically professional suicide and must be avoided at all costs. That's why they're called "everlasting job stoppers." The higher a tattoo creeps above your collar line, the better your chances of being unemployed. That's just science.

But you wouldn't get one of those because you're a hot, young twentysomething in the market for a trendy tattoo. Tattoos aren't just for ruffians anymore; they're for anyone who wants strangers to think they're cool. Maybe you'll get a feather on your rib cage like your favorite model on Instagram. That trend might seem cool now, but just like the barbed wire on your uncle's bicep, that feather may become a super-lame time capsule of a regrettable era. A lower-back tattoo used to be sexy; now it's called a "tramp stamp." Don't let your tattoo be this era's parachute pants.

Tattoos above the Neck

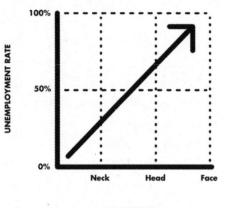

PLACEMENT

Just Do This

Look, if you're going to do it and you've assessed all the possible risks to your social and professional career, then get a tattoo *you* actually like. In the end, your tattoo is only impressive to someone else if they're looking at it. After that, it's just a drawing on your body that you have to live with. Get something you can see yourself enjoying for the rest of your life, and if you can't think that far ahead, don't get one. If you're still up for it, come into the shop with your own drawing or idea to ensure you're getting something truly original. And if you're getting a tattoo with words, *spell check*, *spell check*, *spell check*.

COMMONLY MISSPELLED TATTOOS
BELIEVE = BELEEVE
REDEMPTION = REDEPTION
LIVE YOUR LIFE = LIVE YOU'RE LIFE

Don't rely on a guy who gives tattoos for a living to know how to spell "Redemption." Just make sure your tattoo remains a fond way to remember a specific time in your life, not the reason you can't take your shirt off at a public swimming pool.

Getting a Haircut

Perfect World

You're looking a little shaggy. Sweeping hair out of your eyes was sexy for a few weeks, but now it's more of an inconvenience than a fashion statement. It's not the '70s anymore; you need to get a haircut. Good news: you live in the Big City, and you can't throw a bottle of Suave conditioner without hitting a trendy salon. After leaving that temple of trims, you'll feel revitalized, as if those few extra inches of hair dangling from your head were holding you back from discovering your fullest potential as a human being on planet Earth. Now with a newfound zest for life, thanks to a perfect haircut, you land that promotion, get hit on by a hot bartender, and understand the inner workings of the universe.

Get Real

Maybe that will happen. *Maybe*. But a perfect haircut is rare, and achieving enlightenment because of a haircut is close to impossible. Remember that a hair salon, like any other service industry business, has the human factor, which will result in a different customer experience depending on the day. Like, say Crystal just broke up with her longtime boyfriend. Consequently, her tear-filled eyes could cloud her vision, and she could accidentally snip your bangs off. Or Stewart's car could have gotten towed the night before, resulting in a cut from a guy who wants to work off some rage and whose fists are angrily clenching sharp objects. Or there's that stylist who's terrible but somehow hasn't gotten fired yet. Just because it's someone's job to cut hair doesn't mean he's good at it.

Or you might luck out and get someone who's fantastic, but she treats your hair as a blank canvas, ignoring your requests not to take too much off the top. She'll dig in, boldly going with an asymmetrical cut because it's hot in Prague right now. You'll hate the style—*hate* it—but you'll still have to pay because "an artist" cut your hair.

Just Do This

To walk away with a scalp full of luscious locks, go online and follow these steps:

1. Find a salon in your price range on Yelp.
2. Look for multiple positive reviews for one of the stylists who works at that salon.

3. Call that salon and request the highly praised stylist.

Once at the salon, be as clear as possible with the stylist about what you want. Maybe even bring in a picture, or pull one up on that fancy smartphone of yours. Also, avoid talking about politics when sitting in the chair. Keep conversation light and pleasant. You never know people's political leanings for sure, but you might find out when Bianca razors your neck red after you complain about ObamaCare.

And everyone likes a good deal, but haircuts are something in life where you should pay a little more. If "Super" or "Cuttery" is in the business's name, you might be walking out with a "Super" uncool haircut. Save some money by not buying a couple lattes and apply that extra cash to protecting your daily attractiveness.

Hair Pun Salons to Avoid

A CLOSE SHAVE   **MAKE THE CUT**   **SHEAR VALUE**

If you follow all this advice and *still* somehow leave the salon with an uneven mop top, no biggie. The great thing about hair is that it grows back. You'll get to give it another try soon.

Mani-Pedi

Perfect World

You still can't believe Trisha is getting married. In less than a month you're going to officially lose your first friend to the bliss of matrimony, but until she says "I do," you're still the most fun, beautiful girls in the world. And to celebrate, you're getting all your friends together at the salon so you can bond just like the old days. Time to get pampered. Time to have fun! It's time for a mani-pedi!

Get Real

If you can make it past the fear of catching something from those shared cuticle cutters, a good mani-pedi is a great way to relax and empower a group of women. While it feels good to have your extremities buffed and detailed, if you're not careful, a trip to the nail salon can end up feeling like a real nail-biter.

This is such a fun day to catch up with the girls again.

Or at least it would be if you all got to sit together. Busy adult schedules leave Saturday the only day for all of your friends—and every other girl in town—to hit the salon, so your group is split up among stressed-out moms, texting teens, and rich ladies who won't quit blabbing about how their third marriages aren't working out the way they demanded in the prenup. These outings are always more fun when you can all gab together, so always make sure to call ahead and ask for a reservation. And make sure to update the salon with an exact head count. The only thing worse than being split up is having a late addition forced to sit by herself.

Oh well, the problems of the group will quickly melt away once your nails are the center of some serious attention. You're getting a manicure *and* a pedicure *at the same time*! Like a princess, you're being waited on literally hand and foot. Speaking of feet, you'd better hope they're not digging out your fingernail beds at the same time they scrub your feet because you are so ticklish that you won't be able to control… *Ouch!* Too late, you just got stabbed in the finger when your feet got touched.

While your nail technician may offer you a halfhearted apology, you know she's not to blame because you should have given her a heads-up. Ticklish feet are cute when you're five, but it's unsettling when you're paying a stranger at a nail spa. If this is a problem for you, always tell your nail tech so she'll know to handle your work in stages.

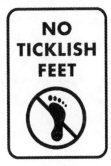

Wow, that color looks really good. One hand done and you can already tell it's going to match your new summer dress perfectly. Or at least it will be close. Oh snap, if it's too dark you're going to have to be that jerk who makes them start all over because *you* selected the wrong color. Better hope you have some extra tip money in your purse to compensate for that momentary color blindness, or you can be sure your nail tech is going to tell everyone in the break room how hard you are to work with.

If you don't want to get stuck with the new girl next time you come in, snap a quick photo on your phone of the color you're trying to match, then show the picture at the salon to get the right color the first time. If you *do* choose unwisely, chill out. It's not like you're getting something permanent like a tattoo. Eventually your nails will grow out. Don't ask for the nail tech to do it over. No one likes doing the same job twice, especially when it involves touching feet.

Just Do This

The mani-pedi is a fabulous opportunity to have a good time, bond, and transform your nail beds into magnificent pieces of art, but just because someone else is doing the work doesn't mean you don't have responsibilities. If you come prepared and can show them exactly what you want, it's easier to relax and enjoy living like royalty. It also doesn't hurt to tip well to ensure you'll be treated with the same grace upon your next return. Which will probably be moments after you start digging around in your purse for that box of Tic Tacs.

Personal Trainer

Perfect World

Eighteen…nineteen…twenty! You did it! Never in your life did you imagine you could bench that much weight. And you were right; you could never have lifted that much *alone*. But thanks to Travis, you're under the supervision of a superman and you're getting bigger, faster, and stronger than you've ever been before. Most importantly, you're getting fit *and* having fun doing workouts you've never heard of. *TRX inverted pull-ups? Sumerian one-leg dead lifts? Hip flexor lateral accelerators?* You wouldn't have figured out these sweet moves on your own. It's all thanks to your boy T-Rav. Time to grab another tank top and front-load a protein shake because you're about to get jacked in another session with your friend and personal trainer.

Get Real

Before you finish that set of hip flexor lateral accelerators, take a quick peek in the mirror and see what your pal T-Rav has you doing. Yeah, he can call it whatever he wants, but it sure looks an awful lot like you're dry-humping that poor medicine ball right there in front of everyone. People may get the wrong idea seeing you do that while T-Rav keeps calling you a "pussy" in his outside voice, so you'd better request a quick cooldown and think this over.

Personal trainers can be a big help in getting your high school varsity body back, but if you're not ready for the rigors of elite fitness at the hands of a possible crazy person, you may be in for a daily session of painful physical and emotional humiliation.

You wanted to jump back into the fitness game and really take it up a notch with a personal trainer. And boy, the guy the gym assigned you is a beast. No, seriously, he is a beast of a person. Not only is he huge, but he also uses war cries and animalistic grunts to motivate you. It's not fun. He doesn't care that you haven't worked out since sophomore year of college. His mission is to get results, and he's going to get them even if it kills him or you, or both. So get ready to be inspired like his college football coaches inspired him: by telling you you're worthless until you do that last rep.

While this method may be beneficial for certain people with a background in elite sports, it may be unappealing for anyone who is not okay being berated by other adults. When you speak to a gym representative, make sure to emphasize your level of fitness experience so you're assigned a personal trainer who will motivate you in a way that will make you actually want to train.

You are not into all that bro shit, so thankfully you've been given a personal trainer who doesn't yell. Or get in your face. Hell, he doesn't really do anything except text. He texts while you fumble through a set of squats, and texts instead of spotting you while you try to bench more than your own weight. Just as a personal trainer who pushes too hard can be counterproductive, so can a trainer who doesn't do anything. You don't have to pay for that. If this happens, ask for your money back. Then walk up to any meathead between sets and ask how you can get as big and strong as him. You'll get way more advice than you ever wanted (seriously, they won't shut up about it), and best of all, it will be free.

Just Do This

A personal trainer can give you the one-on-one guidance that will help you get in shape and stay healthy as you begin your adult life, but he or she can also be a frustrating, demeaning money hole that turns you off to fitness in general. Don't let one person dictate your desire to get active. When you sign up for training, resist the urge to go big and buy a year's worth of sessions. Start by buying a small package of four to six sessions. That way you're not financially bound to a program you hate.

And if you're assigned a personal trainer you don't like, dump him or her and get a new one. Complain to the staff until you find the right trainer for you. Requesting a new person may feel uncomfortable, but you paid a lot of money and deserve to find a good match. The trainers will understand. Or they won't. Who cares? Focus on your health, and don't worry about what T-Rav thinks of you. Friend or foe, there's a good chance he's still going to call you a "pussy."

ROMANCE

Picking Up Girls

Perfect World

You're at the bar, single, and so ready to mingle. You get a fresh drink in your hand and spot a hottie who has no idea what's about to hit her. Normally, you wouldn't know what to say to a ten like this, but luckily you thumbed through your notes from episodes of *The Pickup Artist* before you came and you're ready to "neg" your way right into that girl's heart (and blouse). You tell her she's "really not *that* pretty" and act disinterested, and suddenly as if on cue, she's dying to find out why she's so basic. Game. Set. You mention the cool neighborhood you live in and… Match. That, boys, is how a man picks up a woman.

Get Real

Correction: that is exactly how a man picks up a woman on VH1. Newsflash, this is real life and that *Pickup Artist* bullshit isn't going to cut it. That may have worked back in 2007, but this is the future.

Contemporary Pickup Artist Names

It's going to take more than power moves to attract the strong, independent woman of today. You may have to (gasp!) be yourself!

Pickup lines are a great place to start if you want to remain alone for the rest of your life. They are the social equivalent of announcing you're a sex offender. No matter what you might have had going for you, those words cannot be unheard and there is no way to come back from them. Instead, just try introducing yourself. It may be awkward at first, but at least you're far more likely to be respected for your confidence than rejected for your creepiness.

You think you're a cool guy, so you try to impress her with a story from your trip to Asia, and you tell her what it's like at your kick-ass design job. Oh, oh, oh, and how hard you work out with your personal trainer, and your rad loft warehouse apartment…and that's when her eyes roll and she looks for someone else she can actually talk to. Instead of only talking about yourself, try asking about *her*.

Show that you want to get to know someone who's not you, and you'll be amazed at how much faster her defenses go down.

Be interested, and just maybe she'll be interested in you back. Compliment her on her earrings, or ask if she has a suggestion for what drink you should get. You know, have a conversation. It's what humans do, dummy. Try it. And if she's in a big group, acknowledge her friends and maybe even include them in your conversation. If you get her friends on your side, you're on the fast track to those seven magic numbers.

Just Do This

The only thing that smells worse than all that cologne you're wearing is desperation. No girl wants to be with a guy who tries way too hard, so stop trying to figure out some secret to picking up girls. Work on being a kind, lighthearted guy that people enjoy talking to. If you can focus on being a good listener and make her feel like she's the only person in the world you want to get to know, you just might discover she feels the same way about you.

Picking Up Guys

Perfect World

You get dressed in that sexy little number you just bought. Put on a couple striking accessories, some killer heels, and you are looking *fine*. That's the goal, because you and your girls are going out tonight! Once inside the bar, you'll see a cute guy across the room. You two will lock eyes and you'll give that smile that says, "Come on over, baby. Let's get to know each other." He'll approach you, transfixed by your feminine wiles. As easy as flicking a light switch, this guy is turned on. You just have that effect on men. It is *so easy* to pick up guys.

Get Real

Actually…it is. It doesn't take much to pick up a guy. Guys are simple creatures. When guys play games, they're football and basketball, not psychological chess. The problem with guys—and it's a big one—is that guys are incredibly dense.

They have no idea if a girl is into them or not. Remember, guys are simple creatures. So you need to let that guy at the bar know you're interested in him, because most likely he's clueless. It sometimes has to be as blatant as "accidentally" bumping into the dude you like and saying, "Oh sorry, I become a total klutz around cute guys." Guys are *that* dense. Seriously.

Or maybe the guy noticed you and thinks you're cute, but he doesn't want to walk over because he's too nervous or doesn't want to get rejected. And you don't want to play the "total klutz." If neither of you ever makes the first move, you will have a Cold War of attraction. You both want to smash into each other but are too afraid of the repercussions if you're the first to initiate. While historically this was a good approach to political diplomacy that saved millions of lives, it's a terrible idea for picking up a guy at a bar.

No one will die if you walk up to a dude and say, "Hi, I like your shirt." And that dude will be relieved you made the first move. Oh my gosh, do you know how much easier it would be for guys if girls made the first move? Soooo much easier. It's *terrifying* to approach an attractive girl like you, especially if you're surrounded by more girls who are almost as attractive as you. But it's terrifying for you too. Everyone's afraid of each other, which is stupid. Go up to the person you want to get to know, start a conversation, and move physically closer to him as the conversation continues. Now, if you do all this and he *still* doesn't understand you're interested in him, then you are not dealing with a guy. You are dealing with a boy.

Three Types of Males

Boy	Guy	Man
Emotionally stunted. Has no idea about the world around him. See: early Adam Sandler films. In extreme situations, also known as "Douche." Wants to have sex with you.	More mature than a boy. Still trying to figure it out, but on the road to adulthood. Has glimmers of maturity if you wait long enough. Wants to have sex with you.	Has life together. Comfortable with self. No longer in "blackout drunk" era of life. Wants to have sex with you but will treat you like a lady before, during, and after.

Just Do This

Approaching a dude is the fastest way to make your intentions known, but if you don't feel comfortable walking up to him on your own, grab your girls and make it a team effort. The only thing a dude likes more than talking to a girl who approaches him is talking to multiple girls who approach him. Now you can find out what he's like from the safety of your crew. If he's cool, your ladies will know and let you two have a private conversation. And if he's a dud, you have backup to whisk you away. Lionesses hunt in packs because they know there's strength in numbers. So go out there and take that big, dumb animal down. He won't even see it coming.

One-Night Stand

Perfect World

Awww yea-yuh. You're funny, you're charming, you're not trying too hard, and you're genuinely interested in the cool girl you're talking to. You are totally picking up someone at the bar! While you were planning on just asking for her number, you can tell by the way she's looking at you over her peartini that you may not have to. This girl doesn't want to go on a date next week; she wants to go to your place *tonight*.

After another round of drunk making out by the bathroom, you both say good-bye to your friends over the roar of their approval. While your vision might be blurry, it won't keep you from seeing this exciting development to the end. Even a blind man can read Braille, and you're going to read this girl's Braille all night long.

Get Real

Whoa, check out that hot stranger sleeping in your bed. She is, like, really hot. Like, "go to brunch together, buy a French bulldog, and get married forever" hot. Better get your mom on the line and tell her the good news: you finally found "The One." Oh, "The One" is waking up, and she looks terrified. "The One" is frantically trying to get her dress on and find her shoes because she wants to get the hell out of there. You just had a one-night stand, and although you felt a strong connection, this girl is desperately looking for a connecting flight away from you.

Class : None		**Regret**Airlines
From	**To**	**Time**
Your Place	Anywhere Else	Now
Excuse	**Did you forget:**	
Feed my cat	□ Clothes/Bag □ Phone □ Keys	

Sorry to break it to you, but in almost every one-night stand, someone's going to make it weird, and this time it happens to be you. She doesn't want to grab brunch or get married. She doesn't even want your phone number. She wants to get out of your shitty apartment so she can try to forget the mistake she just made. Alcohol makes people do funny things, and last night it made you think you had a lasting bond with that hot, cool girl. Just like your buzz, your dream date is gone, and now you're left with your head spinning.

Getting your heart broken sucks, but not as much as bringing a crazy person home and breaking hers. Under the haze of alcohol, everyone is the right kind of crazy, but in the morning you can discover some people are the *wrong* kind of crazy. This girl may be a nut, and what you both did in the throes of drunken, awkward passion sealed the boyfriend deal for her. You're *her* "The One," and she's not going to let you go. (Oh yeah, and she knows where you live now.)

Don't bother making an excuse for why she's gotta leave in the morning. She already explored your apartment while you were sleeping and made you breakfast in bed so you two have time to plan out your day together. These may sound like crazy actions, but you'd do the same if you were the one into her.

Just Do This

Next time you're in this situation, before taking anyone home, ask a sober person if this is a good idea. Decisions like this are always better made without wearing drunk goggles and may require a pair of sober eyes to help you make the right call.

SOBER EYES = **DROGGLES**

If you do go for it, make things less awkward in the morning by just being honest and sharing your feelings. That may feel weird, but the situation will be far less confusing and uncomfortable when you both know exactly where you stand. Who knows? You both may get on well and this could be the start of something special. Just remember to agree on a better story when people ask how you two met.

Online Dating

Perfect World

You can't find a significant other *anywhere* in the real world. The coffee shop, the Laundromat, the library, the museum. Not even singles night at Drunkee's.[1] Never fear—the Internet is here! Yes, the place that provides you with unlimited free porn is also the place where you can find someone to date. And with those fancy matching algorithms all the dating sites use, you'll find a wonderful person to date as quickly as ordering a new Brita filter from Amazon. Those fiber-optic cables spanning the nation speed up Internet connections, but now they will speed up something even more important: love.

Get Real

You *might* find someone through online dating, but it sure won't be quick. The Internet has lowered the bar for entry

---

1. As of writing this, Drunkee's is not an establishment that exists. However, several bars do exist which should totally be called Drunkee's.

in everything, including online dating. Just as everyone with a guitar is trying to be a musician on YouTube, everyone with a profile picture is trying to be your soul mate on an online dating site. Even with those fancy matching algorithms, you're going to run into these "YouTube musician" types, but if you don't mind sorting through *a lot* of "guy with guitar" photos, you might find someone decent.

Also, before you join the ocean of people with a dating profile, know what you want to get out of online dating. If you're looking for a relationship, be careful which sites you join. Some of them are going to be like online glory holes, where if you're brave, drunk, or desperate enough, you can find a hookup *tonight*. If you *do* want to give anonymous sex a whirl, then grab a rando and bone your heart out. But if you're looking for something more, then only join sites with a proven matchmaking success rate. That way you can ensure your connection goes viral in a way that doesn't include painful urination.

Just Do This

Even though there are some bizarre, boring, and unattractive people out there, that doesn't mean they're all like that. You can still find some good ones on dating sites. *You're* on there, aren't you? And besides, dating has always been hard. More than half of all books and television shows exist because of the trials of dating.[2] Online dating just adds different problems to the mix. But remember: it also adds different benefits. Before, you couldn't wear your pajamas in your living room and check out a hottie. Now you can. So grab a bowl of ice cream, boot up your laptop, and start sifting.

---

2. *This is an approximation unfounded in hard facts.*

First Date

Perfect World

You met a terrific person [at work/in a public place/ online/through a friend], and now you two are going on a first date! Butterflies. So many butterflies. This will be the start of something wonderful. You'll have sparkling conversation over cocktails and laugh when you both admit you haven't seen [a very popular movie]. You thought you were the only one! As the moon rises in the night sky, you'll stare into each other's eyes and wonder if the person sitting across from you could be your significant other for life. Maybe it's just the butterflies, but your feet are barely touching the ground.

Get Real

It'd be so great if your first date was going to be one to remember. Unfortunately, it may not be. There's a distinct possibility that your first date will suck. See, the thing about first dates is they're the first. Just like being the first person to put his tongue on a frozen pole, most first *anythings* aren't a happy memory. A first date is essentially a job interview. No, it's less than that. A first date is one of those "informational interviews," where you meet with a random employee from the company *before* the job interview. You talk yourself up and let the employee know you exist and want a job, so if she likes you enough and a job opens up, she'll keep you in mind.

This other person having a cup of coffee across from you said yes to a meeting. That's it. You have no idea *why* she said yes. It could have been because she thinks you're going to be friends. Or if you work in the same industry, she may see this as a networking opportunity. Or she could be cheap and know she'll get a free meal out of you. Heck, she might just pity you and feel bad saying no.

Sure, there's also the chance that she might actually like you. But even if she likes you, who's to say how *much* she likes you? She might still be iffy about the whole thing, but all her friends are encouraging her to take more chances, so she says sure, why not grab a coffee? And she has to run some errands in that part of town anyway, so she might as well take a break for an hour or two while her laundry is in the tumble-dry cycle. Most likely she doesn't know much about you, so this first date is your chance to convince her that you're worth a second actual "interview" for the position of "datable person."

But don't push it. Don't be in pitch mode. Very few

people enjoy spending time with a desperate salesperson. But you also can't be aloof and distant on the date, trying to play it cool all the time. That's the tricky position you're in on a first date. Basically, be the best version of yourself, the version that will make people think, "Wow. I could really see myself dating this person." And keep the first date light. This isn't the time to share your grandma's dying wish or talk about immigration reform. You'll have plenty of time to dive into more dicey topics on future dates if this one goes well.

FIRST DATE CONVERSATION TOPIC NO-NOS:

Your ex

Politics

Religion

Family medical history

How poor or rich you are

Just Do This

Usually, you're going to get a good sense of your compatibility with a person on a first date. If you don't vibe, move on. You'll either hit it off or you won't. No sense wasting your time with something you both know isn't going anywhere. The good news is there are plenty of funny, exciting, wonderful people out there to date if this one doesn't work out.

So just go on the date and see where it leads. Spend some time with a fellow human for a couple hours. Even if you don't end up marrying this person, you might still have a fun time. And if the date *does* suck, it'll still be one to remember, just for different reasons. You've got yourself an awesome new story to tell your friends.

First Kiss

Perfect World

It's your second date, and the evening's winding down. You've had fun, and based on the number of times she's laughed (you've been keeping count), she has too. On the walk back to her door, you pause a moment and look deeply into her eyes. She reciprocates. You gently clasp her hands, pull her close, and go in for your first kiss... The *clip-clop* of a horse-drawn carriage goes by as the Eiffel Tower lights up in the distance.

Get Real

Man, that would be awesome if you were smooth or romantic or in Paris. Alas, you're just an American-based dude out on a second date with that girl you met at Trisha's party. While you two have been hitting it off and you think you've earned a couple chuckles, this isn't the time to go all Jack Sparrow on her and steal one as soon as you find the opening.

Pirates get hanged for stealing booty, so if you ever want to hang with this booty again, you'd better slow down and think this through.

Sure, you've heard women are attracted to a romantic guy with a touch of bad boy attitude, but if you just go in there and try to kiss an unsuspecting woman, your roguish assertiveness can appear real rape-y, real quick. Yes, a woman is going to want you to initiate that first foray of intimacy, but she's going to have to give you the subtle go-ahead. Captain Jack Sparrow may be the greatest pirate in the Caribbean, but he still knows to look before he leaps.

When she gives you the go-ahead, *then* it's time to make your move.

But this doesn't mean you got the go-ahead for a mouth-to-mouth free-for-all. Unless your bold gesture caused her heart to stop beating (relax, Romeo, it didn't), she doesn't want a standing CPR session. She just wants you to kiss her gently. So ease up on the urgency and try to relax. And if more than twenty minutes have gone by since the last time you shaved, be mindful that your face is now covered in 60 grit sandpaper. Beard burn certainly has its place in the steamy throes of passion, but rubbing her face raw in a public setting is ultimately going to leave you both feeling uncomfortable. Oh, and that tongue of yours stays in your mouth *period*, until she initiates. Unexpectedly throwing a tongue in a mouth is only cute when dogs do it.

Just Do This

A first kiss is always hard. That's why it comes with so much pressure. Just remember that a confident first kiss can transform you into Prince Charming, but an unwarranted attempt will leave you looking like your dad's single friend who tries to pick up chicks at the bowling alley. Just be cool, wait for your moment, take it easy, and *be cool*. And unless you are hanging upside down thanks to a radioactive spider bite, please lay off the fancy stuff.

There will be plenty of time for that crap once you've proven you're not a creep. If you do it right, this will be remembered as just the first kiss...not the last.

Sending Nude Pics

Perfect World

You and your new crush have been getting pretty close over the past few weeks, and you can't wait for your big date on Friday night. He's so cute, and smart, and caring—oh, and did you mention cute? Ugh, you are so into him it's embarrassing. He's so cute! God, is Friday ever coming? Yes, you're both busy right now, and you've agreed to wait until Friday to ensure you'll both focus on your work, but the only thing you can focus on right now is him.

You know what? Maybe you should give him a little taste of what you have in mind for the next time you see him. Sure, you could text something sweet like an emoji heart, but you don't want to come on too strong. Hmm…maybe just snap a completely nude photo of yourself and send that? Totally better than a cartoon heart. There's no way he can misinterpret boobs as a plea for commitment or a lasting relationship. Good move. Send him boobs!

Get Real

Cool. You just sent a naked photo to your (hopefully?) boyfriend *and* everyone else he knows. Watch the news. This stuff happens all the time. Yes, you only sent it to one specific person you "trust," but how certain are you he's not going to send it to someone and then *that* guy sends it to someone else, and on down the line to more and more untrustworthy people?

Nude photos in the digital age are like twenty-dollar bills. Those babies are going to change filthy hands for a long time. Best-case scenario, a handful of people see that picture. Worst-case scenario, you end up on one of "those" websites where one of your dad's friends says, "Hey, Stan, that looks like your kid." That's the thing with digital images these days. You just never know where they'll end up.

Even if you are in a real relationship with someone you trust, that doesn't mean your relationship will always remain a happy one. Unfortunately, breakups happen all the time, and if your relationship ends poorly, you're not going to want your ex to have an archive of your most intimate moments. Vengeance moves fairly fast in the twenty-first century, and showing your goodies to his entire frat would be a terrible, irreversible side effect of a lover's quarrel.

Okay, but yeah, you're not dumb enough to just text

these tit top secrets. You'll put the pics in your password-protected cloud-based gallery so *you* can regulate who sees them. That's a strong defense—until someone decides to hack your cloud's servers and makes everyone's photos public. This is a wild time for online security, and some hackers just want to prove they can take down corporations with a couple keystrokes. Do you really want your boobs to go public as a result of someone's political statement? You don't have to be famous to get hacked, so think twice before putting your twins out there.

Just Do This

Instead of sending nude pics, how about you don't? There are far less risky ways to show your desire for intimacy than exposing yourself to the world. Like, you could just keep it text-based. Yeah, it's not as sexy, but it is 100 percent safer because you can always deny a text. "Damn it! Sorry! I left my phone on the table and my roommate wrote that!" Boom. The explanation might be unconvincing, but you still have plausible deniability, something politicians use on scandals far worse than nude pics. Keep your most intimate moments for the right someone who deserves to see you naked in person.

Valentine's Day

Perfect World

It's February 14, and love is in the air. The most romantic day of the year is finally here: Valentine's Day. You've been dating that special someone for a couple weeks now, so this year you're finally going to be a part of the festivities. You can't wait to see what he has planned for you. Maybe it's a heart-shaped package delivered to the office; maybe it's a candlelit dinner at a restaurant where it's impossible to get a table. Whatever it ends up being, it will make you feel good to know someone cares about you deeply. Forget what everyone else says; you are proof that true love exists.

Get Real

You may be in for a painful Cupid's arrow right in the ass if you expect all of that stuff to happen. You don't live in a fairy tale, as much as Valentine's Day commercials try to convince you otherwise. You went on a couple dates with someone. So what? That doesn't mean you're together, and that *definitely* doesn't mean you should expect flowers or chocolates. He bought you popcorn at the movie you saw. That's the level of gift giving you're at right now.

This holiday is for people who are, like, suuuuper serious. If you haven't had "the talk," you're not there yet. You may just coincidentally be dating someone in mid-February, but that doesn't entitle you to celebrate Valentine's Day together. That's like assuming there will be snow on Christmas. It makes sense from a calendar standpoint, but it's not guaranteed.

And if you *are* suuuuper serious with someone, that doesn't mean you should expect a storybook Valentine's Day either. This holiday is not a test for your significant other to stress over. You shouldn't be prepared to flunk them if they fail to pull off the perfect evening and the perfect gift. Why are you testing the person you care about anyway? You're not a university. He wants to date you, not enroll as a freshman. If your boo gets you a present on Valentine's Day— even if it's a gift card to TGI Fridays—that's a kind gesture. See the good intention in his gift giving, not the fact it should have been a tennis bracelet. Besides, TGI Fridays has some solid potato skins, and you two can share them *together*.

If your boo doesn't get you the perfect present, you should not banish him to the doghouse. His affection for you is not directly linked to the quality of gift he gives. His affection is linked to actually wanting to spend time with you.

You might think your significant other doesn't have his shit together because of a bad gift, but you don't have it together either. Like, in life. Be thankful that someone in the world is okay with enduring your youthful failings as you stumble your way into adulthood. That's a pretty big deal.

At the very least, your partner should wish you a happy Valentine's Day. Anything above that does not come standard in the relationship contract.

Just Do This

Stop assuming you deserve things on Valentine's Day. Sure, maybe Stacy got two dozen long-stem roses delivered to the office from her sweetheart, but you're not Stacy. Getting those roses does not make her any better than you, even though she will try to make you feel that way. But that's Stacy, and you know how Stacy is. If you're just starting to date someone and you'd like it to be more, don't force him into doing or buying you anything because it's February 14 and the Jared commercial told you it should happen.

Nothing puts the brakes on a budding relationship faster than thrusting obligations onto a dude who's just starting to like you. And if you *are* with someone in a real, caring relationship, he'll make you feel good about yourself and your relationship that day. That doesn't mean he'll buy you a yacht, but he will show you how much he cares in whatever way that means to him.

It's much easier for Cupid's arrow to hit your heart if your arms aren't folded.

Making It Official

Perfect World

You've made it past the first date, second date, third date, and more. This is starting to feel like something real. You're growing closer to this other person. You're always talking to your friends about how great he or she is, and you're positive this special someone feels the same way about you. So you take a deep breath, look him or her in the eyes, and say you want to make it official… Then cue the brass band, set off the fireworks, and link your Facebook profiles. You are now in a committed relationship with someone who's fantastic! The whole world needs to know: you've made it official!

Get Real

While making it official may be what you want when you define the relationship, or DTR, you'll never know for sure which way a DTR talk will go until you have one.

Be advised, DTR is very different from the also commonly used dating acronym DTF, which refers to when you're horny and down to…you know. Chronologically, in most cases you are DTF before you want to DTR. But who knows? Maybe you have incredible willpower and are holding out until you DTR. Whatever the order, right now you're about to talk about what "this" is between you and your partner.

OTHER CONFUSING DT ACRONYMS

DTI = Dress to Impress

DTL = Doing the Laundry

DTB = Dance to Beyoncé

DTD = Drench the Dog

(as in liberally applying
condiments to a hot dog)

And sadly, the other person might want something completely different than you when it comes to "this." You might be projecting what *you* want your partner to want out of it and ignoring all the huge signals indicating that he or she wants otherwise. The fact that she's still posing with hotties on Facebook? Those must be her cousins. And that recent picture of her making out with someone in the club? She must be *really* close to her cousins. The fact you're happier with incest than the idea of nonexclusivity means you definitely need to talk some stuff out.

There is a huge downside to having a candid discussion about your relationship: the results might not be what you want to hear. They might, in fact, be the opposite of what you want to hear. While you saw these past twelve dates as magical and the beginning of a burgeoning love, your partner could have seen them as a "fun time" that won't lead to anything substantial. And that sucks. So much. But ultimately, if you both don't want the same things, then why waste each other's time?

Maybe your dating partner just isn't ready yet. Maybe you brought up "the talk" too early, like on the second date. (Don't do that. No one enjoys that.) If you don't get the answer you want at this moment, that doesn't mean you won't get it eventually. It just means you might have to be patient. But if you've been patient over weeks or months and nothing is changing, maybe you should move on. It's not your job to wait for someone to change. You have to know when to hold them and know when to fold them.

Other Life Advice from Country Western Songs

1. If searching for the devil, try Georgia.

2. Hearts occasionally become achy-breaky.

3. Some of your friends will be in low places.

Just Do This

Real talk can be scary, especially when you're telling your true feelings to someone you really care about. If that person doesn't feel the same way, he or she could completely destroy you. You're exposing yourself to heartache. But heartache is better than living in a fantasy where you assume this person is your significant other and he or she is not. Defining the relationship is the best way to see where you and your partner are. It could be wonderful, just like you hoped, but you'll never know until you talk. So dive in and discuss.

Romantic Weekend Getaway

Perfect World

You've been in a relationship for a while now. You've both said "I love you," you've celebrated a milestone anniversary, and you only stop holding hands when one of you has to go to the bathroom. It's time to go on your first romantic weekend getaway! Nothing takes a relationship to the next level like spending an entire weekend together in an exciting new place. Another city, a camping trip, an exotic destination—doesn't matter. You two will be together, and your romance will grow.

Get Real

Or it will end. Badly. You know how steel is forged in fire? That's what a trip with your romantic partner is: a white-hot flame setting your relationship ablaze. If it's meant to be, you'll come out of it stronger and oxidized. If not, you'll be left cracked and brittle. A trip with *anyone*, romantic or not, is a trying experience. Even though a vacation should be relaxing, some unforeseen inconvenience inevitably comes up. In those moments under pressure, you see a person's true self, and once you do, it can never be unseen.

You might have been together over six months, but have you ever been in a car with this person for six hours? No? Then you do not know this person. Don't worry. Since you'll be together for every minute of this trip, you will get to learn *everything* about your partner, especially all the annoying things. This weekend getaway is really a weekend seminar on "Your Partner's Faults as a Human Being."

YOUR PARTNER'S FAULTS AS A HUMAN BEING

SEMINAR SCHEDULE:

9:00 · **KEYNOTE**

10:30 · **BREAK**

11:00 · **HIS OR HER LACK OF AMBITION**

12:00 · **SINGS WRONG SONG LYRICS**

1:00 · **LUNCH**

2:00 · **WHAT'S WRONG WITH MY MOTHER?**

3:00 · **WHAT AM I DOING HERE?**

4:00 · **CLOSING REMARKS**

This trip threw you into a different locale. You're outside the safety and comfort of home. So you'll cling to the one stable thing that you associate with home: your partner. But somehow, with the backdrop of a different locale, you'll start to see different mannerisms of your partner too. Like how he's a bad tipper. You really never noticed before, but that's because you didn't see him buy stuff eight times a day. And did he just make a racist comment about your server?

Are you dating a racist person? You must have heard him wrong. Nope, he just made a disparaging comment about migrant farm workers. Huh. You never noticed these things back home, but that's because you never had the chance to look. You were too busy being in love. Well, roll up those sleeves, 'cause love gets tested on the road.

No doubt you'll be drinking more than usual since it's a vacation, so topics long kept quiet will make their inaugural debut on this trip thanks to alcohol. Nothing's off the table after a fourth margarita. That's called "honesty time." You never thought your partner was jealous of your ex; now you know she is. And she thinks your friend Drew is lame? Why'd she have to bring Drew into this? To level the playing field, you'll bring up your own inner thoughts and fears about this relationship, which won't help anyone. Jeez, you weren't supposed to fight. You were just supposed to have a couple days together, eat good food, and screw like crazy. Well, be sure to pack aspirin, because between the hangover and traveling back home after honesty time, your head's gonna need it.

Just Do This

A romantic weekend getaway will amplify everything in your relationship. No one likes to be scrutinized, but it's going to happen on a trip. Maybe—hopefully—you'll only see the shining beacon of love and light you knew when you were dating. And all those mishaps on the trip will be things you'll laugh at as you reminisce while surrounded by your grandkids fifty years from now. But it could easily go the other way. That's not entirely bad though, because this trip made you realize you weren't dating the right person, and that's always good to find out before you start shopping for engagement rings. Hey, at least you got some cool Instagram pics.

Moving In

Perfect World

Your relationship survived that romantic weekend getaway. You two still bask in the constant love of each other. But it's not enough. There are still times when you are unable to bask. These unbasking moments torture you at night, when you're sleeping alone in a bed that feels too big without your partner. This needs to change. You want to see her more. Nay, you *need* to see her more. You want to wake up to her beautiful face every morning for the rest of your life. It's time to ask her the big question. No, not marriage. That'd be crazy! Ha-ha-ha-ha-ha-ha! Oh man, yeah, even *you* know you're not ready for that. No, you're going to ask to move in together.

And why shouldn't you? It'll be everything both of you want from this relationship! Moving in before tying the knot is the new thing for trendy, career-minded young professional couples like you. Millions of parents will purse their lips in judgment of your choice to live in sin, but you don't care! You're in love! Plus, "living in sin" isn't a phrase people use anymore, unless they're performing a Tennessee Williams play. No, you're in a "domestic partnership" now, and boy does it feel good.

Get Real

You can call your arrangement whatever you want, but you're in *deep*. This is serious. You're technically not married, but…basically you're married. It's the two of you living together under the covenant of a lease for as long as you both shall tolerate each other.

But that's what you wanted, right? You wanted to play house. So get ready for Target trips to buy throw pillows, discussions about accent wall colors, and debates on anything and everything your domestic partner finds on Pinterest. Since you're not getting married, you don't have to plan a wedding, so that energy gets put into sprucing up your nest. You're skipping past simpler decisions like what kind of wedding cake you should have to whether you can live without a dishwasher and if carpeted rooms are okay. The level of decision making is all backwards.

You're not married, but you're going to fight like you are. Someone isn't doing the dishes? He didn't hang up his jacket? She wants to have a night out with her friends without you? Your domestic life is practically turning into a sitcom, but there's no laugh track to tell you when it's funny. Remember when you used to have roommates? Well, your partner is your new roommate. Yes, you have more ready access to sex

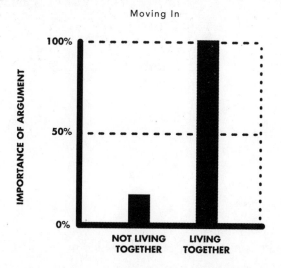

now, but you also have to deal with all those normal room-mate things. Like compromise. And understanding someone's feelings. And working through the hard times. It's *exhausting*.

Just Do This

The problems you had in your relationship before you moved in together aren't going to magically go away once you share the same address. Hopefully you're moving in because it's actually working out pretty well between you two. If not, moving in to try to fix your problems is a less extreme version of having a baby to save a marriage. Both are bad ideas. At least with moving in, the lease is month to month, not eighteen years.

Moving Out

Perfect World

Your partner is *awful*. It's not going to work out, and now you're just wasting each other's time. How did you ever think there would be a future with this person? You should have realized it before you signed a lease together. Oh well. It's time to move out and move on. You're going to feel so much better getting the hell out of here.

Get Real

You *will* feel better, but only for a very short time. Like, the time it takes to slam the front door and drive to a friend's apartment. You'll think of all those irksome traits your partner has. She thought she was so much better than you. Like that patronizing look she gave when you ordered your meal at the trendy restaurant. Like she could order so much better? Ugh. So obnoxious.

Then that song comes on the radio…the same song that

played in the bar when you two stole that pint glass. Petty theft never seemed so romantic. This seemingly innocent recollection will trigger the depression spiral: fears of dying alone, getting too old to have kids, having to find another place to live—that's just for starters. Depending on your psychological fortitude, you will experience days, weeks, or months of this, both stewing in regret about what you could have done differently and terrified of an unknown future with no one by your side.

Even though every friend and dating website tells you not to, you'll go on social media and scroll through all of your ex's pictures. Oh, she changed her profile picture. And it's of her wearing that one outfit you said you didn't like. That's *so* like her. She's trying to get to you. You should text her about it.

It doesn't matter. You're not with her anymore. Move on.

Did he lose weight? And does he have a new, stylish haircut? Man, he looks *good*. He's probably rebounding with someone hotter than you. Just taking some rando every which way in the bed you two bought together at IKEA.

It doesn't matter. You're not with him anymore. Move on.

At your lowest point, you'll convince yourself that you two should get back together. She wasn't so bad. You had so many good times! Why did you break up? You don't even remember anymore. You can make this work.

No you can't. You moved out for a reason. Trust your instincts. On some very deep level, you two have irreconcilable differences. And those differences won't change on the second go-round. You're not missing the person. You're missing the feeling of being with someone. You're missing companionship and security and sex. Oh, the sex was so good. And consistent. Now you're down to high-speed Internet and an incognito window on your browser. Well, lock your door and learn to love yourself, 'cause that's all you'll be getting for a while.

Just Do This

A lot of relationships are not going to work out. That doesn't mean you shouldn't still try. You're also going to die some-day, but that doesn't mean you should avoid living before that happens. Breakups suck. They really do. But you learn from them and grow stronger and better prepared for your next relationship, thanks to all that grief you experienced. Moving out is hard, but if you never move on, you'll never be able to move on up.

LEISURE

Coffee Shop

Perfect World

Your entire Sunday afternoon is wide open. Why not spend it at your local coffee shop? You'll savor a latte art–dappled mocha in an overstuffed chair next to a roaring fire and listen to accessible folk music wafting through the speakers. What a great way to spend a lazy afternoon.

Get Real

Yes, it *is* great, which is why everyone else had the same idea as you. It's going to be pretty hard to get that overstuffed chair you want. Most likely, you'll be standing in the corner, eyeing every customer with a seat and getting pissed they're taking so long to savor their latte art–dappled mochas. *You* should be the one doing that. You'll get to hear Joni Mitchell over the speakers, but her velvety chops will only remind you of the fact you are not luxuriating.

With each passing minute, your drink will deflate more.

Or you'll be drinking it already. Either way, by the time you beat that selfish pregnant lady to the only vacated seat in the place, your drink will be finished or cold. Somehow, room-temperature cappuccino foam doesn't taste that good.

Then there's the whole bathroom situation. Sure, you might miraculously get a seat, but then you have to pee thanks to that coffee. So now you have to mark your territory with some disposable item you brought to let those new customers standing in the corner know, "Hands off my chair. I'm still using it." You need to use a worthless item to do this, like a notebook or a sweatshirt. If it's something like your laptop, then you have to introduce yourself to a stranger and go through the rigmarole of asking if they can watch your laptop. And let's be serious, no one really wants to watch your laptop. Even if they say they will, who's to say they *actually will*? They didn't come here to stare at another person's computer while that person's taking a leak.

Speaking of laptops, why did you bring yours to this coffee shop anyway? Hopefully you just brought it to surf the Web or check your email and not to work on something important. Because you are going to get very little actual work done crammed into this java clown car. You're not going to write the Great American Novel at this place. And finishing that spreadsheet for work probably won't happen either.

If you really want to accomplish a substantial work session, try looking up a coworking space in your city. They charge money for you to become a member, but because you're paying money, it could actually force you to get some work done. Plus, they usually provide free unlimited coffee to their members, and it's a heck of a lot easier finding a place to sit than at a coffee shop.

Just Do This

Coffee shops aren't all bad. The waiting in line is bad. Sometimes the service is bad. But the people watching is always good. And if you have to stand for half an hour until a seat opens up, you'll have plenty of time to *really* people watch. Like, stare at each person until one of them gets the picture and leaves.

Flea Market

Perfect World

You love fake old things. That's why you put the old-timey filter on every Instagram picture you post. Well, if you go to a flea market, you can buy *real* old things, no filter needed. And since it's a flea market, you're bound to find some great deals on those real old things. Your keen eye will spot an unassuming and exquisite prize buried under a pile of water-damaged posters. All you have to do is look. Get some cash, clear out your trunk, and drive on over. You're going to find that diamond in the rough!

Get Real

You are not going to find a diamond in the rough. It's not likely at least. That's like finding a needle in a haystack. If diamonds or needles were as common as the overused phrases mentioning them, you'd be set. But flea markets are not full of clichés. They are, however, full of junk.

Lots and lots of junk. Imagine a hoarder taking everything he owns out of his house and trying to sell it. Now imagine hundreds of hoarders next to one another all trying to do the same thing. And then imagine hoarders wandering among the hoarders looking for more things to hoard. That's a flea market.

THE FLEA MARKET FORMULA

a flea market = (your kooky aunt's basement)^2 + (money)

Most of this stuff is worthless, and deep down, even you know that. But you still go, hoping you'll find that one great table or rug or antique that will complete your newly redecorated living room. You might find something decent in your search, but you're holding out for the jackpot. Just like with Vegas, you've heard the success stories of a flea market. That lady who found a Tiffany lamp in a wooden crate. Or that dude who bought an oil painting for twenty bucks, only to discover it's a priceless work of art. Those stories keep people like you coming back. Also like Vegas, you probably won't be one of the success stories at the flea market, but it doesn't hurt to try. At least with a flea market you're not pouring your money into a slot machine.

Just Do This

The joy of a flea market—if you can call bending over for hours and touching bacteria-ridden objects "joy"—is the act of searching. You need to be Zen about it. A flea market is about the eternal hope of finding something spectacular, but when you don't find something spectacular—and you probably won't—you should not be upset. You signed up for that. But maybe you *will* find something or meet someone or have some other wonderful experience while you're there. You never know what you'll find, and that's the fun part. If you really, truly want a specific item, stay at home and find it on eBay. Leave the flea markets for dreamers and people with up-to-date tetanus shots.

Porn

Perfect World

Your roommates are gone and won't be back for a couple hours. You've caught up on the shows on your DVR and you're not in the mood for reading. You *are* in the mood for something else, though…something a little *sexy*. Something called porn. Well, boot up that broadband Internet and pull your pants down. It's time to give yourself a hand.

Get Real

Headphones on and secure, you watch the video, transfixed, as people more attractive than you contort themselves into positions you could never pull off. And as soon as it started, it's over. Not the video. The video's still going, but you're done. Depending on your level of sexual guilt, you'll either immediately hate yourself or merely clean up. Maybe somewhere in the middle. But the moment with yourself and the world of porn has reached its climax, and you need to go about your day again.

Just Do This

Porn is a fantasy. It's a release from the boring real world you have to deal with all the time. You know that. But after too much porn, the fantasy of it can start to mess with how you view that real world where you spend most of your time.

Porn is one of the key reasons why people go through life expecting everything to be wonderful. Because everything works out in porn. Everyone is sexually satisfied and people are always up for *anything*. It's a sexual world of make-believe. Real maids don't wear fishnet stockings, and most professors aren't DTF during office hours. At least not the ones you would actually want to have sex with.

NON-DTF CAREERS	DTF CAREERS
nurse	prostitute
school girl	
construction worker	
deliveryman	
foreign language tutor	

And do you really want to have sex for hours straight? Like, seriously *hours* rubbing things raw down there? And would you want to have sex on and in weird places? Those kitchen granite counters look really uncomfortable and cold to bone on, and the dirty bathroom in the back of a dive bar doesn't seem like the best idea either. But the more you watch these videos, the more you compare your life to them, and you get more and more disappointed. You never had sex with your banker when you applied for a loan, and it *kills* you. You shouldn't live in that world. Weekend visits are one thing, but don't buy a time-share.

You probably will never meet someone in your life who looks like a porn star, and if you somehow do, he or she most likely will not want to have sex with you. Ever. If you hold out for the surgically enhanced nymphomaniac of your dreams, you're going to end up sad, alone, and sexually un-fulfilled. Instead, enjoy the real, attainable humans around you. They might not look like the girls in porn, but they're better than having sex with your own hand.

Your Birthday

Perfect World

Happy birthday! You survived another year! These last twelve months have been pretty crazy, right? You had some low points when [insert conflict at job] happened, and then [insert friend's name] started [insert unacceptable friendship behavior], but you got through it all and are better for it. Now it's your birthday. Everyone you pass on the street today will exclaim, "Happy birthday!" Adorable old men in the park will tip their old men hats at you, the highest sign of respect. And you'll get so much free stuff. Everywhere you go, just birthday swag up to your eyeballs. Yes, this day is all about you. It will be the best day of your year and *of your life*.

Get Real

Maybe to you. To everyone else on planet Earth, it's just another Wednesday. When you order your morning coffee, you'll have to tell the barista it's your birthday, and you might get a forced "Happy birthday" back, but she really wants to spit in your face. She had to open the store at 4:00 a.m. and she has a paper due tomorrow. Your birthday doesn't get her jazzed up since it's not *her* birthday.

That barista doesn't know you, but your coworkers do. They'll surely do something big for this special day of yours, right? Doubtful. There won't be balloons and streamers and a bugler announcing your presence as you enter the office. This is still a Wednesday, and they all have work to do. You'll try to shoehorn a mention of your birthday into a conversation, like, "Sorry I'm a little late. It's my birthday today," and your desk mate will offhandedly say, "Oh, happy birthday," as he finishes a spreadsheet. If you're lucky, Jill from HR will feel bad and send out the intern to quickly get some grocery store cupcakes. An hour later, you'll have an unceremonious dirge rendition of "Happy Birthday" sung to you in the break room by employees who would rather be working (which is saying something).

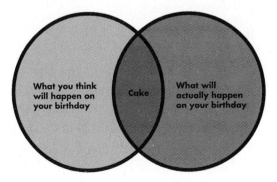

Whatever. That's just work. Your coworkers aren't your real friends. What you're really looking forward to is your big birthday party at that swanky new mixology bar in town this coming weekend. You consciously scheduled the party on the weekend to make sure there would be a huge turnout. And there totally would be…if it weren't for the rain. And the fact the big game is on tonight. Stupid athletes and their weekend games!

You shake off the low turnout, because who cares? It's your birthday and you're drunk, and you are getting laid tonight! All this free alcohol lets you say whatever you want, so you're going to talk to every gorgeous person in the bar. And then you're going to scare them all away with your cavalier free spirit. Maybe if you hadn't taken that last shot with your roommate you'd still be in the zone. Instead, you're now sloppy drunk, and no one comes back from that.

Just Do This

For your birthday, you don't need attention or a big blowout celebration. Just be happy for what you do have: people in your life who care about you. They might not buy you a cake, but there are more important things than cream cheese frosting. Most likely, your closest friends will make the effort to show up to your birthday festivities. And as long as your core group of buddies shows up, that's all that matters. Plus you'll have a mountain of Facebook wall posts to read throughout the day. Desiree from high school didn't have to type "Happy birthday!" But the fact that she did is pretty cool.

Your birthday is just another day of the year. Enjoy each day, especially the other 364.

Adult Softball League

Perfect World

They said you didn't have it anymore. That you'd lost your athletic touch. That you're a has-been. Well, this has-been is looking down the barrel of a full count in the bottom of the ninth with a runner in scoring position. As that softball leaves the pitcher's mitt, arching above head level and into the batter's box, you block out all the haters and focus on one thing: your love of the game. The sound of aluminum hitting softball snaps you out of your spiritual trance, and you watch your hit going…going…gone! And the crowd goes wild.

Get Real

All four members of the crowd go wild: Trevor's girlfriend, Dan's wife, your roommate, and that guy walking his dog.

They're thrilled this game is finally over. Your teammates echo their enthusiasm because they can go home too. Welcome to the world of adult sports leagues. No one really cares about the game, and all the infield home runs on this planet aren't going to change that.

Back in school, you were at the top of your game, so you needed the latest gear to help you take it to that next level. Today, you're an office worker in an entry-level position. No one's going to notice your Ultramax baseball cleats or your hundred-dollar glove. They're only going to notice you can't afford to buy a round at the bar afterward. So save your money for what's important (drinks) and just get cheap gear that works. Even if you have a top-end bat, the pitcher is still going to throw to you underhand.

As the game progresses and tempers start to rise, do everyone a favor and shut the hell up. There is absolutely no arguing with the officials in coed softball. Although it's played like baseball, there is an unspoken set of rules geared toward hot-headed jerks like you to help keep this fun. The biggest rule on the list is "Don't Be an Asshole." Did an official make an "incorrect" call? Just shut up and don't be an asshole.

Did a girl not touch third when she made her way to home plate? Just shut up and don't be an asshole. Did your captain put you on the bench to let a new friend get a start? Just shut up and don't be an asshole. Everyone is willfully risking injury to waste their precious leisure time with you for *free*, so the last thing they need is you being all competitive and making this not fun. So if you start to get mad for any reason, see above for what to do.

Just Do This

Coed softball is supposed to be fun, so let yourself enjoy it. Strike out, goof off, and have a good time. If you need more than that, quit and join a competitive league. Just be careful, since those guys will probably be just like you.

The Beach

Perfect World

Sun's out, guns out! Crank up the Beach Boys, grab your trunks, and throw on some shades. You are going to the beach! Better hope none of these bikini blonds have heart conditions, because you and your glistening six-pack are about to get some pulses pounding. Get ready for a full day of fun, sun, and beach babe buns. This party don't stop till the tide goes out. Surf's up, dude!

Get Real

Yes, the surf is up and crashing all around you, desperate to reclaim all life that once crawled out of it. Today, that just happens to include you. You are literally in over your head, so you'd better buoy yourself to this life preserver of advice before the Coast Guard is sent out to rescue your social life. The beach may appear to be Mother Nature's VIP section, but just like the actual VIP section, this magical place may cost you everything.

Before you hit the water, ask yourself, *Am I a good swimmer?* If you hesitated with your answer, then don't swim out far. This isn't the pool at the Holiday Inn Express. This is a real body of water, and that current's job is to play for keeps. Nothing is going to blow the whistle on your beach hunny game quite like having a lifeguard drag your bloated carcass onto the sand for a lifesaving CPR rotation. If you don't want your only mouth-to-mouth action to come from some dude trying to save your life, be real about your swimming abilities and only go out as far as your toes can touch.

Maybe it's better to avoid the surf all together and keep your sea legs underutilized right there on the sand. Heck, crack open another cold one and take in more of these hot, hot girls. Some of them are so hot they're hard to see. They're, like, dizzy because you're…getting dizzy… Great. When's the last time you drank something without booze in it? Well, it's been too long and now you're dehydrated. Next to a massive body of water. Toss some water or sports drinks into the cooler with your booze, and remember to slam one in between libations to keep yourself healthy and in the game.

When someone starts that classic "bury me up to my neck in sand" game, just watch and don't join in. This game always starts out as a funny beach activity until some jokester thinks it would be hilarious to put his balls on your helpless face. It happens! All the time. And there's no way to live it down. If you don't want to be the guy who got teabagged, just don't put yourself in that position.

Now, there may be a moment when twilight skinny-dipping becomes a thing, and if it does, just like that teabagging, someone is going to get disrespected. In a big group of skinny-dipping guys and girls, some poor sap's swimsuit is always going to go missing. Don't get left to the mercy of the full moon. When this shit goes down, *you* have to be the one who hides someone else's suit. Yes, it's juvenile and wrong, but it's going to happen to someone—might as well not be you. Before you take the moral high ground, consider how that cold water isn't going to do you any favors downstairs and do what must be done.

Just Do This

A day at the beach can be life changing for better or worse. Ensure it is for the better and take care of yourself. Just as if you were in the woods or in the desert, respect Mother Nature's power. Know the limits of your physical prowess in the water, stay hydrated, and remember to apply and *re*-apply sunscreen. No one wants to make out with a red lobster. If you can take care of yourself in the elements and defend yourself from various balls hitting your face, this could be the kind of day the Beach Boys always wanted you to have.

Hiking

Perfect World

You followed the rules all week. You were at your desk every day at eight and even stayed late a couple times. You've been stuck in traffic, had to circle your apartment multiple times looking for parking, and wasted your Friday night at your coworker's housewarming party. You've had all the civilization you can stand in a five-day period. It's time you got back to nature. Just call yourself Lewis and Clark; you were born to blaze trails into the unknown. So dust off that coonskin cap and don't stop driving until you pass the city limits. The wild is calling, and today you're finally going to answer. Today, you're going hiking.

Get Real

You are like other great explorers in that you are also a human. Outside of that, the comparison gets lost—just like you're about to be on this little nature adventure. Wanting to get in touch with man's undying need to explore is one thing, but escaping the pitfalls of civilization to feasibly fall into an actual pit in the woods is another. Daniel Boone didn't have a nine-to-five for the same reason you're not a real adventurer. He would have been awful at it. So, if you don't want other rescuers to comment on how cool your new hiking shoes look on your dead body, proceed with caution.

Oh, you brought a compass? Well, why didn't you say so? Enjoy yourself out there! As long as you took a bearing from where you left the car, you'll be able to get back in no time...but if you didn't, your fancy compass is nothing more than a useless rotating trinket. It doesn't matter which direction north is if you don't know what direction you came from.

If you don't know how to use it, a compass is as useless in the wild as a Magic 8-Ball. You can shake it all you want, but you'll never get a straight answer.

How lost can you really be? You're just going on an easy hike. So easy, in fact, that you didn't even bring a water bottle. Although getting turned around did leave you in the sun longer than you expected, you're still nowhere near thirsty enough to consider drinking your own pee. That liquidy, thirst-quenching, sweet, sweet pee… No! This isn't an East Berlin nightclub. You are *not* drinking pee! The best way to keep these thoughts from happening is to prevent yourself from getting dehydrated. Only plane-crash survivors and underage girls at music festivals get dehydrated, so keep a full water bottle and your dignity with you at all times in the wild.

Just Do This

Hiking is a great way to find yourself, as long as a search party doesn't have to be called in to help. Plan ahead, bring water, and know where you are going. Pay attention to your surroundings so you can always recognize your way back. If you find that all rocks and trees "look the same," bring a buddy who can tell them apart. Bringing another civilized person with you isn't always ideal when you're trying to escape civilization, but it beats dying alone with a brand-new compass.

Road Trip

Perfect World

Your friends want to hop in a car and drive to [a universally acknowledged fun vacation destination]. Awesome! It's been so long since you've gotten on the open road when it hasn't been your commute to work. On this trip, you and your friends will totally grow even closer and create new inside jokes that will last a lifetime. Pack some snacks and start your engine. Kerouac ain't gonna have nothin' on you. You are going on a road trip.

Get Real

A road trip is about as American an activity as you can do. It's ingrained in America's mythos. Hell, Huck Finn was road trippin' before there were roads. There's something about packing up and exploring this great land that still resonates with us as a nation. But just like some of America's history, you want to forget some road trips. Not all of them are worthy of a monument.

Many factors contribute to making a road trip either an enjoyable experience or one you never want to speak of again. First off, how long is this road trip? That's the big question, because that affects everything. A couple hours in a car is much different than two days. You can handle an annoying friend in a car when it's a day trip, but if you're crossing state lines with a brat, you've got to change your approach. You need to pace yourself differently for a road trip sprint or a road trip marathon. If it's multiple days, try to refrain from talking nonstop. No one wants to hear someone ramble on constantly any more than they want to read your live tweets of the passing billboards.

Some of those billboards will advertise roadside attractions that sound really cool and even have a gas station next to them. You have to stop for gas, so why not go to the roadside attraction too? But if you do end up pulling off to see The Enigma Place or the World's Largest Something, it will rarely be worth the detour. Most roadside attractions will suck harrrd. Approach them as nothing more than an opportunity to stretch or buy patriotic bald eagle T-shirts, which is all they're really good for.

On a road trip, you're also going to use a lot of gas station bathrooms, which will offer relief and an onslaught of bacteria. Pack some hand sanitizer and use multiple seat covers to insure fewer breakouts of hepatitis. If you're supersmart and impervious to glares, you can pull into a motel and use their lobby bathroom. Or just suck it up and contract a disease (free souvenir!).

Just Do This

A road trip could be a fun way to get to a destination, depending on the company. Being stuck in a car changes people, and if you're already not sure about someone before you buckle up, he or she is going to be a lot worse by the time you get where you're going. Know what you're getting into before setting off on the dusty trail. A road trip will let you see a whole bunch of the country that you wouldn't normally see, but sometimes after seeing it, you'll realize why people choose to fly. Most of the country is boring. But with the right people, the right tunes, and the right 'tude, a road trip could turn into something for the history books.

NIGHTLIFE

The Subway

Perfect World

That's it. You're done with driving. The traffic in this city is a disease. A seemingly endless system of clogged arteries hell-bent on bringing both this city's life and yours to its knees. It's time to cure this sickness with the finest remedy your tax dollars have to offer. Remove your quivering hands from the steering wheel, pay a couple bucks, and peacefully glide beneath the darkness of the city. Enough is enough. Tonight, you're taking the subway.

Get Real

A couple paltry bills to go from one side of the city to the other? That's crazy! But not nearly as crazy as some of the people you're about to encounter. We're not talking "crazy" like your uncle who tells funny stories about the '70s, but "crazy" like a guy who thinks he's an actual dog (and he's willing to bite you on the face to prove it). Oh yes, you are going off the rails on an actual crazy train. Although the legitimacy of Dog Man's business may be questionable, he has paid his fare and thus has the right to travel across the city barking at other passengers the same as you. Like being on a tropical reality show, you didn't go down there to make friends, so don't make too much eye contact and keep to yourself. Dog Man may not be up on his shots.

GOOD CRAZY	BAD CRAZY
'70s uncle	Dog Man

Pop quiz: Ever been robbed by a guy with face tattoos? Well, you're about to be. While you might feel like you're a part of the team since you and your fellow passengers are all embracing public transportation together, you are still an outsider here, and everybody knows it. The subway may be the last great unifier of the social classes, but these guys aren't down there to prove social harmony is possible. This is the *real* city here. No one can take the belief in an efficient transit system from you, but they can (and will) take your wallet, so be on your guard at night.

Just Do This

The subway is a fantastic way to get around the Big City, but it can also be a great place to get yourself into trouble. If you take the train at night, stay alert or try to travel with a buddy. Two people can still get robbed together, but at least the odds are a little more in your favor. It's also always a good idea to research your trip before you ride. That way you will be sure to get off at the right stop and avoid any questionable areas.

Night Subway Route

Not everyone on the subway wants to do you harm, but there is certainly someone on every subway who would if you gave him the opportunity. Like the similarly named sandwich shop, the subway can be a cheap and satisfying experience; just be aware of the potential risks in case you can't stomach it.

The Club

Perfect World

You've had a lonely week full of tough deadlines and early bedtimes. It's time to shake it off and meet someone special. The girls are picking you up at eleven, so dust off that gold bandage dress, put on your cute heels, and get your hair looking *right*. Tonight you're going to have fun. Tonight you're falling in love. Tonight you're going to the club!

Get Real

Ha! If you think you're going to find love in a nightclub, your heart's going to be in more pain than your feet from those heels. A group of six dudes in jean shorts have a better chance of getting into the club than love, so don't expect love to be buying you any drinks or (appropriately) grinding on you tonight. But there *are* plenty of dudes waiting inside to try to do that.

Who knows? You may meet someone…if you ever get

inside. The line to get in is about a mile long, and it doesn't seem to be moving at all. Sure, a group of girls is supposed to waltz right past the line and bouncer, but because your friend Mindy thought tonight would be a good night to wear her new gaucho pants instead of a hot dress, your whole group isn't getting in anytime soon. That's not fair, but it's the business model of this industry, so if you want to be a part of it, you gotta follow the rules. When you plan a girls' night, make sure everyone gets the dress code memo so you can take advantage of the misogynistic system and skip the line like pros.

Now that you're finally inside, you see that waiting in line was totally worth it. This place is ridiculous, and since you're looking so cute, you're not going to have any problem meeting a guy...because they are *everywhere*. So many dudes touching, talking, and grabbing you by the wrist to try to persuade (drag) you and your girls to their VIP table. Don't confuse the free drinks from them with genuine attraction. Even if they're not asking for money, the way they're leering at your tight dress makes it clear they want something in return. If you don't feel like spending the whole night dodging some dude looking for a return on his investment, don't accept more than one free drink, and be polite when you excuse yourself to dance to "your song."

The dance floor is where you finally get to lock eyes, smile, and groove your way into some dreamy dude's heart. That is, if he will look at you for more than five seconds without staring at some go-go dancer instead. These massive party clubs always have paid dancers to set the sexy vibe, but good luck keeping a guy's attention when he's within eye-sight of them. Guys are kind of dumb, and they have a hard time focusing when bare flesh is near. You may be tempted to let him get a little handsy to keep his attention, but be careful not to set up his expectations for something physical if that's not your intention. There are plenty more dudes in this place, and maybe one or two even want to give you some non-grope-y attention.

Just Do This

The club sounds like a cool place to meet someone special, but it can quickly turn into a long night of dodging creeps and frustration. Avoid some headaches by only going to clubs where someone "knows the promoter" so you can skip the lines and party in more exclusive sections where there are fewer weirdos to worry about. Also remember that the club isn't always the best place to look for a real relationship with a normal person. If it were, there wouldn't be a large man with a clipboard outside the door trying to keep all the normal people out. Go in with the intention of having fun with your girls while you dance the night away and just leave it at that. It's much easier to spot a great guy when there isn't a strobe light.

The Strip Club

Perfect World

She can't take her eyes off you, and you can't take your eyes off her either. Sure, her body is amazing, but it's those eyes you can't stop staring at. They hold secrets you want to know. In a moment, she's leading you back to the Champagne Room where, alone at last, she tells you her real name. You peel another hundred-dollar bill off your roll and offer to pay for her private services. She refuses, instead telling you she gets off in an hour. From the way she whispered it in your ear, there's a good chance you will too. No, this might not be the Disney version of falling in love, but you have a feeling this storybook romance will end with a happy ending.

Get Real

Whoa. You fell in love at the strip club? Great. So did the guy waiting in the hall, so if you're about done picking out your kids' names, his thicker wallet would love to talk to her next. Sorry pal, but the strip club is not a place to fall in love or expect anything other than walking out with less money than you came in with.

The strip club is a place for your brain to release some chemicals and for you to burn through some cash. And only actual fire can burn through cash faster than the strip club. So keep your wallet and your heart in a cool, dry place because it is about to get real hot in here.

Before you go any further, stop and remember: you are not going into an amoral den of adult entertainment. You are going into a business, a damn good business that specializes in taking money for nothing. Sure, these gals may be dancing alone on a stage without their clothes on, but you're the idiot paying to watch. These women are not the sad women you think you can ogle and exploit; these women are smart, savvy, shirtless business professionals with full, satisfying real lives that don't in any way include you. They don't want to date you, get to know you, or sleep with you. They want to withdraw funds from you and that's it. Let them do their work and save the romance for someone not at their job.

If things heat up and you do feel like paying for a little Champagne Room treatment, keep your cool and don't be a creep. Just like at your office job, if you try to have sex here, there will be consequences. Only here, those consequences will be a bouncer's fist to your face. If you don't want to explain to your dentist why your mouth is full of broken teeth and glitter (he already figured it out), just prevent the preventable and keep calm.

Just Do This

You're not at an auction house, so don't keep shelling out more money in an attempt to "win" something. The only thing you'll win will be a pair of blue balls. Bring the maximum amount of cash you want to spend and stick to your budget. Avoid temptation and outrageous ATM fees by leaving your debit card at home. Buy everything with cash so you can keep to your prehorny allowance, and don't open a tab at the bar because that's where things can really get out of hand. Most importantly, promise that once your money's gone, so are you. Have some laughs, feel pervy, and go home with your dignity and credit score still (somewhat) intact. Ensure that the only boob you see is on the stage and not in your bathroom mirror when you get home.

Karaoke

Perfect World

It's Friday night, and you have a serious need to belt out some rockin' tunes. Timeless classics? Current hits? Could go either way. The one certainty about tonight is *you are going to sing.* You're not one of those people who gets badgered into singing a karaoke song. You welcome it. You've been mastering hits like "Total Eclipse of the Heart" since you were a kid. Well, this ain't your cousin's basement anymore. This is karaoke in the Big City, and your star is ready to be born.

Get Real

Yes, a star is being born…into a cold and ambivalent universe. You may have all the talent in the world, but the people in the Big City aren't at this karaoke place to notice you. The Big City has a surplus of unfulfilled singer-performer types, so they congregate in karaoke bars to get that intoxicating taste of the limelight. Then there are the regular folks who also just like singing. They come out like you because it's the weekend and they want to sing. So grab a seat and rest your vocal chords; you're going to wait a long time.

While you wait, you might as well make use of the bar. Bars serve alcohol, *and you love alcohol!* You can have a couple drinks with your friends. Get nice and loose before your performance. But soon one beer turns into three, and then your kooky, "get the party started" friend hands out shots. Before you know it, you are drunk and trying to harmonize with the dude on stage.

When the DJ calls your name, you don't even hear it. The DJ has to say your name again while a friend excitedly screams into your face before you realize it's time to sing. You stumble your way onto the stage, too drunk to recognize how awful the lighting is making your skin look. He plays your song, you start to sing, and you *own* it…until the bridge comes. How did the bridge go again? You muddle through somehow, impressed at how you handle yourself under pressure. Then the instrumental section kicks in.

This song has an instrumental part? And it's twenty-four bars long?! Now you don't know what to do. So you kind of groove to the music for as long as you can without looking awkward. Turns out, it doesn't take long to look awkward onstage grooving silently to music. When the audience starts to turn, you make a joke about your dancing, but with twelve bars to go, it's clear you picked the wrong song, and everyone knows it.

Just Do This

Public speaking is one of the biggest fears for people, so you're already awesome just getting onstage. Most people would never do that. And when you have the spotlight, you can do whatever the hell you want up there. It's *your* three and a half minutes, so if you want to groove, then groove, baby. Just have fun. You know that phrase "dance like no one's watching"? Well, when you're doing karaoke, sing like no one's watching. Just know that everyone is watching, so give them a hell of a show.

Comedy Open Mic

Perfect World

It's another Wednesday night in the Big City. You could spend it going through whatever Netflix suggests for you, or you could go out there and see what's really going on in the world. You're young and hip, and you aren't going to let an algorithm tell you what to experience. You're going to make the choice completely on your own. Tonight, you're going straight to the source of culture: the back room of that old coffee shop for the weekly comedy open mic.

Get Real

You want to see real people tonight? Well, you're about to. A whole bunch of real, crazy people. Sure, if this were 1967, this coffee shop would be a hotbed of artists showcasing the very best of the new generation. But alas, this is the twenty-first century, and talent is an endangered species. At best, you're going to see someone rant for three minutes before arguing on a microphone with the emcee.

There may be a slim chance you'll encounter the next big thing, but you'll more likely discover how much you miss the polished performers on that show Netflix wanted you to watch. Unless you're Berry Gordy looking to sign some new talent (again, this metaphor takes place in the 1960s), avoid the open mic and go do anything else. Just because you're broke and this is free doesn't mean you have to check it out. In this case, you get what you pay for.

If you *do* go, shit's going to get weird. Like, really weird. A comedy open mic is for people trying to find their comedic voice, but they may have to get through a bunch of molestation jokes before they find it. Guess who's their guinea pig?

And if you believe in the goodness of humanity, do your soul a favor and leave before the end. Trust your gut and take off as soon as you first feel the mood turn. Don't worry about hurting anyone's feelings. No one in there has felt anything for years.

Do not bring a date. Repeat: *do not bring a date.* This is *not* a date spot. Your knowledge of the underground comedy scene may impress her for a moment, but all that will go away when a shitty comedian throws in a little crowd work and asks her how often she masturbates. Yep, that's going to happen. Unless you want to have the world's most awkward ride home, take this off your date spot list and replace it with literally anywhere else.

Just Do This

The comedy open mic is a cool concept in theory, but like eating stuffed-crust pizza backwards, it always ends up feeling wrong. If you want to check out rising talent, go to an actual billed show that lists comedians on the poster. That way you're seeing a show curated by someone who at least partly believes in the performers. You may have to pay to get in, but spending a few dollars on a good show always beats seeing a horrible show for free.

Professional Sporting Events

Perfect World

Your favorite sports team has a big rivalry game coming up, and they're going to need all the help they can get. Odds say there's no way your local underdogs can dethrone these visiting juggernauts, but Vegas bookies forgot to factor in your team's greatest asset: *you*. There's only one way to help your team pull off the impossible, so put on your replica jersey, paint your favorite player's number on your face, and grab your team's colored towel to spin above your head. Your team needs you. You're going to the game!

Get Real

Time out. You're going to a professional sporting event? In America? You better have practiced having patience and a willingness to get ripped off, because just like the athletes in the game, you're about to be tested.

As the "We will, we will *rock you*!" chant echoes through

the stadium, you can't help but wonder if Queen wrote this song in reference to the prices that teams are charging their fans. Thirty dollars for parking (four blocks away from the game), sixty-dollar seats in the nosebleed section. These millionaire athletes can afford it, but you can't. And you won't even be able to see those millionaire athletes from where you're seated.

Luckily you can watch most of the action on the giant Jumbotron screen. A pretty cool innovation, until you realize you just got suckered into paying a lot of money to watch TV with a bunch of strangers. Though you hope they have your best interests in mind, some sports organizations seem to be using trick plays on their fan base.

But you only get upset with faraway seats when you're watching an indoor sport like basketball or hockey. Your *favorite* sports happen in the fresh air, where you don't care about where you sit as long as you have the sun on your face...and on your neck, back, shoulders, and any other skin you've decided to leave exposed. Sure, everyone likes a little color, but too much sun and even if your team *wins*, you'll still leave red in the face. If it's going to be a sunny day, just remember to bring some sunscreen, and if the forecast calls for even the slightest chance of a shower, bring some rain gear. No one wants to look like a wet cat if the camera pans over their section.

If your team wins, enjoy it. Be loud, be proud, but whatever you do, don't direct it at the other team's fans. There's a good chance some of them may have been drinking and would love to take out their team's frustration on the first person to give them the finger. There are few ways to make this day even more expensive, and a trip to the ER would certainly be one of them.

Just Do This

There is no substitute for seeing a game live. But watching a game while saving money in a comfortable setting without the fear of violence is pretty good too. Before you buy your tickets, be sure to give that seating chart a good once-over, and if you can't afford to *see* the actual game from a seat, save your dough. Sixty dollars can buy you a lot at a sports bar, and they don't charge you anything for sitting on the stool closest to the TV. If you really want to go to the game, try taking public transit to the arena, plan for the elements, and think about leaving early if there's any fear of confrontation. By taking care of yourself and planning ahead, you can ensure that the only loser at this game is the other team's captain.

House Party

Perfect World

It's Saturday night and the feeling is right. Another long week at the office down, so time to celebrate by getting crunk at someone's big house in the Big City. You better grab a six-pack of brews and your lucky beer pong hat, because you are going to a house party!

Get Real

Before you kick in the front door and yell "Party!" in some nerd's face, ask yourself, *Am I still in college?* If you answer yes, by all means, take it to the limit. If you answer no, go home and put on some closed-toe shoes.

Sorry to ruin the illusion, Uncle Rico, but you're an adult in another adult's home now, so use a coaster, don't run in the house, and for god's sake, keep your voice down. Just because it's a party at someone's house doesn't make it a house party. There will be no motorcycles in the living room

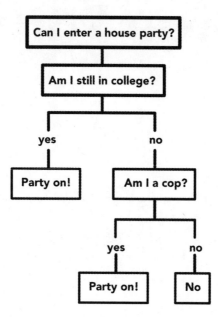

or pizzas hanging from the ceiling. Pretending you didn't hear a couple's whisper fight through the kitchen door is as wild as this party is going to get, so leave that flask of cheap whiskey in your jacket and try not to think about those two condoms burning a hole in your pocket.

Those condoms are as useless here as the small talk you made about the cheese spread on the table. Look around and you'll discover that adult house parties are the couples-only skate of the grown-up world. The only single person's hand you'll hold tonight will be in a dead fish handshake from some other pathetic dude you meet in the living room. Avoid that awkward exchange by always bringing a date or by asking the host if he or she has any single friends that might also be attending. This way you'll have an idea of your romantic odds before you arrive, or you'll have a pretty good reason not to go at all.

If knowing that everyone at this party will have fewer than three drinks the entire night doesn't make it feel much like a house party, you are absolutely right. It's a party at someone's home. It's really more of a *home* party. This will not be a rager or a completely unforgettable night, and that's totally okay. As you get older, you'll come to appreciate these quiet moments with groups of other adults. This transition might feel pretty lame at first, but it is the inevitable decline (or as you'll discover, rise) of adulthood.

So instead of loathing these parties for what they're not, enjoy them for what they *are*: a chance to relax. Sip a glass of good wine, talk to some happy people, and make some new responsible friends with jobs. Enjoy a little civilization for once in your whole dumb life.

Just Do This

If this kind of house party doesn't sound fun, you're welcome to go back to what you know and be the oldest person at some child's rager. Just remember: the only thing worse than being the youngest person at an adult party is being the oldest person at a party where you no longer belong.

Conclusion

Congratulations! You officially know more than we did at your age. But don't get all cocky about it. That would be the exact opposite of how you should act. When you're cocky, you think you know everything. And you do not know everything, which is the way it should be. Just enjoy life as it comes. If you expect less, you actually get more.

Once you're settled into that job you enjoy and have that significant other you care about, you can tell everyone the reason you're so successful was because of this book. You know, tweet about it and do a Facebook post and email everyone in your contacts. Then the entire world will go out and buy a copy, and we'll become incredibly rich and famous. And nothing bad will ever happen to us, all because we wrote this book! (See, we still struggle with this "lowered expectations" thing too.)

Whatever happens, good luck out there in this scary and exciting new stage of your life. Just remember that you can't always control what happens to you, but you *can* control how you react to it. Life can disappoint and it can astonish, and you should prepare for both. Now go out into that big, beautiful world, ready for "good enough." Who knows, "great" might be out there for you too. Just stop expecting it.

Acknowledgments

A *big* collective thank you to everyone who helped make this silly book happen. Anna Michels and Stephanie Bowen at Sourcebooks, Anthony Mattero at Foundry Media, Olivia Gerke at 3Arts Entertainment, Joe Weiner at Miloknay Weiner, and the kindness of Laura Steinel.

A special thanks to the Upright Citizens Brigade Theatre LA for bringing us together. And to the comedic support and friendship of ManCamp's Jay Ashenfelter, Kevin Manwarren, and Timothy Simons. Thanks, Jemps.

Robert would like to thank…

My parents, Mary Ann and Robert, for that kind of love that falls in the unconditional category. And Mom and Dad, Matt wrote all the offensive swears and sex stuff. My big sister, Kristen, for blazing the adult trail first and making my life so much easier because of it. Mark Mavrothalasitis and Davey Vorhes, for being the good kind of roommates. And Andy Sturgeon, Ryan Vukelich, Amanda Dunlap, Thuy-Van Nguyen, Kat Manalac, Jimmy Chang, Jessica Lowe, Jackie Laine, Diana Theobald, Nichole Roberts, Daphne Karpel, Andrew Thomas, Amanda Krieg Thomas, Stephanie Carrie,

Becca Tesarfreund, Dan Millstein, Rachel Lewis, Alex Fox, Annie Simons, and Roxy Radulescu, for being the good kind of friends.

Matt would like to thank…

My folks, Jon and Melinda, for your unwavering support. (Sorry about all the swear words and sex stuff. Robert totally wrote all of that.) Dr. Gerise Herndon, for teaching me to think for myself. Phillip Wilburn, for your ceaseless and often unreturned generosity. Justin Runge, for showing me how funny well-chosen words can be. Claire Cetera, for a woman's perspective. And especially anyone who has ever given me a chance. You didn't have to, and I appreciate it.

Everything funny I ever do, now and forever, is in loving memory of my sister Janna. Sis, your laughter lives on in my heart. Always.

About the Authors

ROBERT BOESEL is a writer, performer, and award-winning filmmaker living in Los Angeles. You may have seen his writing on shows like *Wizards of Waverly Place* and *iCarly*. You have not seen his writing on several projects he sold that never got produced. He hosts and produces the digital travel show, *LAblocks* (LAblocks.com), and cowrites and costars in another creative project with Matt, *Robert and the Magic Mirror*. You can follow all of his creative goings-on at robertboesel.com.

MATT MOORE is a writer, actor, and comedian from rural Nebraska. In addition to performing throughout the United States, he has appeared on television programs including *Conan*, HBO's *Funny or Die Presents*, and *Sean Saves the World*, as well as numerous televised commercial advertisements. He received a BFA from Nebraska Wesleyan University and currently resides in Los Angeles. More Moore at themattmoore.com.

Moore left, Boesel right